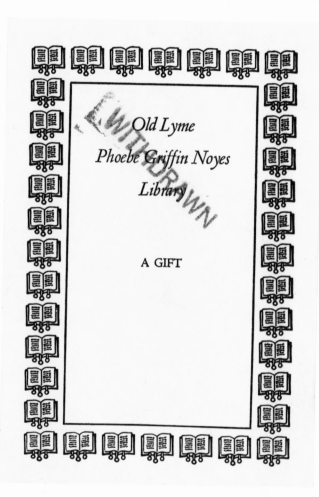

MOTHERCRAFT

by Margaretta Lundell

SIMON AND SCHUSTER • NEW YORK

LIBRARY OF CONGRESS CATALOGING IN PUBLICATION DATA

LUNDELL, MARGARETTA.
    MOTHERCRAFT.

    BIBLIOGRAPHY: P. 153
    1. HOME ECONOMICS.   2. COOKERY.   3. HANDICRAFT.
4. STORY-TELLING.   I.   TITLE.
TX147.L86   649′.1   75-11746
ISBN 0-671-22018-7
ISBN 0-671-22019-5 PBK.

The author gratefully acknowledges permission from the following sources to reproduce material in this book. Any omission is inadvertent and will be corrected in future printings if notification is sent to the publisher.

Denes Agay for "Dixie" and "Yankee Doodle" from *Best Loved Songs of the American People,* published by Doubleday & Company, Inc.

The Art Institute of Chicago for "In the Circus Fernando: The Ring Master" by Henri de Toulouse-Lautrec.

The Trustees of the British Museum for "Rhinoceros" by Albrecht Dürer and for "Enraged Musician" by William Hogarth.

E. P. Dutton & Co., Inc., for "Rice Pudding" and accompanying illustrations from *When We Were Very Young* by A. A. Milne, illustrated by Ernest H. Shepard. Copyright 1924 by E. P. Dutton & Co.; renewal 1952 by A. A. Milne.

Macmillan Publishing Company, Inc., for "The Little Turtle" from *Collected Poems* by Vachel Lindsay. Copyright 1920 by Macmillan Publishing Co., Inc., renewed 1948 by Elizabeth C. Lindsay.

The Metropolitan Museum of Art for "Statue of Sleeping Eros," Rogers Fund, 1943; "Don Manuel Osorio de Zuñiga," by Francisco de Goya, The Jules S. Bache Collection, 1949; and "But, Grandmother, What Big Eyes You Have!" by Paul Gustave Doré, gift of Mrs. John Fiske.

Musée National des Thermes et de l'Hôtel de Cluny for "The Lady and the Unicorn."

The Museum of Modern Art for "Man With a Hat" by Pablo Picasso and "Person Throwing a Stone at a Bird" by Joan Miró.

Naturegraph Co. for Indian Sign Language from *Indian Talk, Hand Signals of the American Indian* by Iron Eyes Cody, copyright 1970 by Naturegraph Co.

Rijksmuseum for "Saint Nicholas Day" by Jan Steen, copyright, Rijksmuseum, Amsterdam.

Simon & Schuster, Inc., for "Skip to My Lou," "The Hokey-Pokey," "Hush, Little Baby" and "Eency Weency Spider" from *The Fireside Book of Children's Songs* by Marie Winn and Allan Miller. Copyright © 1966 by Marie Winn and Allan Miller. And for "The Fox" from *The Fireside Song Book of Birds and Beasts* by Jane Yolen, Barbara Greene and Peter Parnall. Introductions copyright © 1972 by Jane Yolen. Arrangements copyright © 1972 by Barbara Greene. Published by Simon and Schuster, Children's Book Division.

Western Publishing Company, Inc., for "Pop! Goes the Weasel" and "Ring Around a Rosy," from *The Golden Song Book,* arranged by Katharine Tyler Wessells. Copyright 1945, copyright renewed 1973 by Western Publishing Company, Inc.

To the women of America, in whose hands rest the real destinies of the republic, as moulded by the early training and preserved amid the maturer influences of home.

—The American Woman's Home
*Catherine E. Beecher and
Harriet Beecher Stowe, 1896*

And to my resident muse, my son, Erik.

Contents

MOTHERCRAFT

MOTHERCRAFT

Introduction

Since first becoming a mother, I have grown more and more dissatisfied with the quality of my own mothering and that of mothers around me. With our children, we are conscientious but nervous, we try hard but are rarely spontaneous. We have no solid inside reservoir of know-how and confidence.

The self-assurance of American mothers has been seriously undermined in recent years. More and more, women have been bombarded by the often conflicting opinions of child psychologists, pediatricians and early-learning educators. Women's Lib has also complicated the mothering role. The Movement has convinced many women that to be nothing but a mother is to be a failure. Such a mother then cannot help but resent the supposed cause of her failure: her child, her children. The resentment that sets in only takes her further away from her mothering core.

But the problem goes back further. There is a serious lack of instilled moth-

ering knowledge in this generation of mothers. Women are educating themselves well about pregnancy, birth and often breast-feeding, but that is as far as they go alone. Within hours after hospital delivery, new mothers realize that the living beings thrust into their arms are little-known quantities.

Panicked and disoriented, we are suddenly aware we were not taught the craft of mothering. Our mothers knew how to cook real oatmeal for the three-month-old, embroider a smock or make a dandelion chain for the toddler. They were taught the craft, but few passed it down. Though they knew the old ways they had lost the conviction that anything "old" mattered.

The World War II generation of mothers is the missing link with the past. Even before their time, the chain was weakening, but mothers after the war fell prey in vast numbers to the Age of Technology. Commercial entrepreneurs assaulted them. Gerber, Walt Disney, Mattel and many other companies convinced those young mothers that to be modern and efficient, they should buy rather than make.

Sociological changes also worked against these women. Postwar families grew smaller and smaller; daughters had less and less chance to watch their mothers take care of younger sisters and brothers. Also, the nuclear family structure excluded grandmothers, great-aunts and others who used to contribute mothering information. Even women's education got in the way. Mothers became obsessed with their daughters' homework. Night after night, year after year, they insisted on neat geometry assignments rather than sitting with their daughters for an hour to sew.

For our children and ourselves, we have to find a way to keep the benefits of twentieth-century education, technology and change while also recapturing the older, slower sense of mothering calm. In this book I have tried to set down classic mothercraft tools, most of them safely rooted in the pre-World War I era. The recipes and household suggestions call for few prepackaged aids—they begin at the beginning. The samples of old songs, rhymes, stories and art forms are widely varied but dependable, well-anchored and in general of better quality than much of what is being offered today. In the Playtime and Nature chapters, I emphasize things to invent and do with a child that cost little, that will make a parent's time with a child more fruitful, and that will give the child a sense of creating on his own.

There is no chapter on games in the book. Because most of what a young child enjoys takes on the quality of a game anyway, I chose to plant game ideas within the chapters on music, rhyme and so forth. Games with complicated rules can confound a young child and make him resent his mother's superiority. Since there is strength in numbers, I think formal games work better with teachers and groups of children. However, children differ. If your child wants to learn Parcheesi at age three, go ahead and teach it to him.

Fathers are becoming increasingly involved in child care, and the title of this book is not meant to exclude them. A willing father can use anything suggested here. However, since most young children are still being looked after primarily by mothers, I address myself to women.

Mothers should not look at this book as a collection of antiques designed to bring back the good old days. There was much in late Victorian mothering that was maudlin and destructively moralistic. I admit I have weeded out the extremes of the "good"-versus-"bad" concept of child-rearing in that era. The best of the 1900 world was a peaceful sense of family continuity. That aura of contentment is what I wish for us to find again.

The last thing I hope for is to push mothers into doing more for their children. The old, basic ideas put forth here are meant to help a mother save her energy and yet have more of a sense of accomplishment at the end of a day. Even more important are the seeds each mother can add to this garden. We can reach back into our childhood and family past and unearth whatever crafting tools of our own give us each the most personal confidence and joy.

M. LUNDELL

Little children in both England and America have always been taught the rudiments of education at home, as a matter of course. The mother, the aunt or the older sister usually was the teacher. Thus the child began his learning naturally: he scarcely knew he was being taught.

Some self-distrustful mothers now object that they cannot teach. But there is no single plotted path. With the right implements, any mother can encourage the spontaneity of learning.

Once started, the child learns many things fastest by himself. "Teaching" can actually interrupt the momentum of personal thought.

A mother gives a clue. The child draws out the thread, tracing his way through the labyrinth by himself. When he finally arrives at the center, he is alone and triumphant.

—Home, School and Vacation
Annie Winsor Allen, 1907

GOVERNMENT OF CHILDHOOD

The infant at birth contains a germ of all that is great and good. Education is simply the process of drawing out and developing dormant energies. The child's teachers and governors are the parents. They cannot escape this duty if they would, and a large share devolves upon the mother.

If a mother governs entirely by sole, bare authority, by frowns untempered with smiles; when her conduct produces in the hearts of her children only a servile fear instead of an obedient affection; when accidents raise a storm, and faults produce only a hurricane of passion in her bosom; when offenders are driven to concealment and lying in order to avert unduly severe corrections; when the mother interrupts innocent enjoyments unnecessarily; when, in short, she shows nothing of herself but the unhappy tyrant, can we then expect the child to flourish in such soil? No, unless we expect the tenderest house-plant to thrive amidst the rigors of eternal frost.

At the opposite end of the scale are the parents, particularly mothers, who delay the application of coercive measures too long. The first months and then years of a child's life glide away quickly; the mother scarce knows when she should have begun to govern her child instead of having him govern her.

If a child has been accustomed to obey from infancy, there need be no contest for power. The yoke of obedience will generally be light and easy. Just as important is for a mother to be always on her guard and allow no encroachments on her own prerogatives.

Often discipline is abortive. It is administered at a proper time but is relaxed just short of success. No correction should be commenced that is not completed there and then. One completed piece of discipline is worth a hundred abortive efforts.

Love is the essential element of the parental character. The human mind is so constituted as to yield readily to its kindness. Men are more easily led to their duties than driven to them. 'A child,' says an Eastern proverb, 'may lead an elephant by a single hair.'

In all their conduct, let the parents blend the lawgiver with the friend, temper authority with kindness. Let them act so as to convince the children that their laws are holy, just and good, and that to be so governed is to be blessed.

—Maidenhood and Motherhood
John D. West, M.D., 1888

The Child's Body

RECIPES

The strength of the child depends largely on the food given him when he is too young to select for himself.

... Admittedly, kitchen work is hard.
　　　　　　　　　　　　　—The Home and Its Management
　　　　　　　　　　　　　Mabel Hyde Kittredge, 1917

The feeding of small children has been controversial for decades, and the controversy goes on. Should a child "clean his plate," or just go as far as he wants? Should he be fed a hamburger supper early, so his parents can dine in peace later on, or is the ritual of everyone eating together important?

　　Many nutritionists now believe that small meals eaten more than three times a day give the body greater energy. Children seem to know this instinctively, needing their midmorning snack and afternoon "teatime." I respect their instinct. However, I do think at least one relaxed meal each day with everybody in the family is a reassuring pattern for children. During family meals, children need not be catered to individually. They can be taught to try the adult menu.

Snacks and drinks between meals are a particular problem for mothers: what to give a child that will be nutritious but won't spoil his appetite for lunch or dinner. Daily and hourly, we have to fend against Kool-Aid and Toaster Pop Tarts —cheap, instant foods especially invented to entice children. The makers of white bread advertise constantly, but there is no cartoon animal on television to lure our children to dark breads or sesame crackers.

Aside from the nutritional aspect, constantly depending on prepackaged and frozen foods robs a child of a learning experience. Stirring canned green beans is not very interesting. But if a mother is snapping real beans, she can show the child the stalk end, how to break off the tips and snap in the middle. The helper may decide to become a bean thief, popping uncooked pieces into his mouth when she isn't looking. He offers one to the cat, or builds a log house of beans. He laughs and learns. Even though he is slowing down the process, his mother laughs with him.

Food-fixing is not an invented playtime. It is real. You will have gotten something ready for dinner and had a happy sharing time with the child. Constantly cooking with a child would be exhausting, but the sharing times are irreplaceable.

I am not a health-food addict, but I do believe in starting with the raw product as often as possible. It helps a mother expand her art of cooking, and it helps a child develop his palate. The sooner a child is given homemade oatmeal cookies and a glass of eggnog, the easier it is to keep him away from supermarket garbage. The system at home, started early and held to consistently, is what really matters.

A small part of this chapter is given over to quasi-medicinal calmants for a child: camomile tea, warmed honey and lemon, and so on. These few entries are not meant to replace antibiotics, but they may help a mother to wait and judge the situation before calling the pediatrician. There are times when small children are just cranky and tired and want to know that their mothers have ways to comfort them. Any mother knows that when a child's complaint is persistent she should go ahead and get professional help.

But the main focus here is food. The recipes are meant to encourage mothers to make custard instead of buying chocolate pudding in a plastic container. After the first few times, making custard becomes a habit, and habit is half the fight. Eating can be a healthful, peaceful and special time, though for many children and parents, it means battling. I hope the suggestions here will reinforce women's attempts to slow down the household mealtime pace and will help them enjoy nourishing a family.

DRINKS

Lemonade

INGREDIENTS
½ cup lemon juice (approx. 4 lemons)
⅓ cup sugar
grated lemon rind—optional
2½ cups water

TO MAKE
Combine all the ingredients in a quart jar and shake. If it is too sweet for your taste, add the juice of another lemon. If it is too tart, add more water or a bit of sugar. If you want to make it pink, add a little grenadine or a few drops of red food color—not maraschino cherry juice, which is laden with chemicals.

You can triple or quadruple the recipe leaving out the water and have pure syrup on hand. A fourth of a cup of syrup per glass, with water and ice, can be made up when needed. However, citrus fruits lose vitamins with time, so the smaller amount used more quickly is healthier.

Iced Tea

Some children love iced tea in the summertime. Others hate it. If you're going to try it, make the real thing instead of the expensive, instant variety.

TO MAKE
Iced tea should be stronger than hot tea because of the ice dilution. Bring 4 cups of water to a boil. Remove from heat and add 6 teaspoons loose tea or 6 teabags. Let it brew no more than 5 minutes. Strain, or remove teabags, cool and store in container.

Variety is fun for children, so serve the tea in a small glass with ice, lemon juice, a little sugar (minimum), a lemon slice or a cocktail cherry, a spoonful of lemon sherbet, or a cinnamon stick as a stirrer.

Children love to pour out of small pitchers by themselves. Serve the tea this way, or put out small pitchers of lemonade, limeade or orange juice and tell them to add to the tea as much as tastes good to them.

Clear Soup, Hot or Cold

Save all the juices from cooking vegetables, even potatoes, for two or three days. Keep pouring the juices into a single quart refrigerator jar.

Pour in a saucepan. Add a beef or chicken bouillon cube and perhaps some noodles, heat (until noodles are soft), and serve. This is especially good for a sick child who can eat only a little at a time and who needs protein.

Without noodles, this soup can be heated with a bouillon cube for taste, cooled, and served to the child as a cold drink.

Eggnog
One Serving

INGREDIENTS
1 cup milk
1 egg
1 tbs. sugar

TO MAKE
Heat the milk without boiling. In a drinking glass, beat the egg with sugar. Add a few drops of vanilla. Add the warm milk to the glass and stir.

—The Health Care of the Growing Child
Louis Fischer, M.D., 1915

RANDOM NOTES

REFRIGERATED FOODS
Much of what your child drinks and nibbles on between meals depends on what he is used to finding in the refrigerator. By the time he is three or four especially, and wants to "do it by himself," have some of his favorites at the front of the refrigerator. This takes a little calculated planning, but the effort is worthwhile.

–lemonade, fruit juices, milk, cold clear soup, in containers the child can pour from himself (and with a designated cup for him to use). Not carbonated drinks
–yogurt in individual containers
–radishes, carrot and celery sticks in water (to keep them crisp)
–cheese slices

–leftover meatballs (the child may want catsup)
–hard-boiled eggs (if you're very lucky)
–slices of whole-grain nut or raisin breads
–cherry tomatoes
–melon balls (provide toothpicks)
–apples, pears, peaches, plums, grapes (any of which you may have to wash, or teach the child to do it)
–oranges, grapefruits or lemons (which you will have to cut or peel)
–custard or junket in individual cups

NON-REFRIGERATED FOODS

Again, teach the child early that his (healthy) favorites will be close at hand.

–small boxes of raisins
–nutritious cookies
–bananas
–cheese sticks
–protein-rich crackers, which you can teach the child to enjoy with cream cheese. (If you have the energy.) Add olive-slice eyes and a pimento mouth. These special fixings can also be put on top of the darkest, most wholesome breads. Commercial white bread need never be brought into the house.
–sugarless gum and candies

I knew a mother once who put out bowls of raw oatmeal for her two- and three-year-olds. They ate it with their hands, hungrily. A tray under the bowls simplified clean-up.

FROZEN FOODS

For children's lunchtimes or supper-before-the-grown-ups, there are freezer tricks. Buy hamburger meat and make it up into individual patties. Wrap, label, freeze and days later throw into the frying pan when needed. Buy economy packages of chops, chicken pieces, and minute steaks for the same purpose. Thaw the food before mealtime or cook it frozen over low heat. This system can save the day for a harried mother or an anxious baby-sitter.

SNACKS

Chicken Noodle Soup

Teach your child very early (as soon as he can drink from a cup or use a spoon) to enjoy homemade soup. It is inevitably more nutritious than anything out of a can.

INGREDIENTS
1 whole chicken
1 carrot
1 onion
noodles (a generous handful)
salt

TO MAKE

Into a pot of boiling water, put whole chicken. Add carrot (minced). Add onion (minced).

Remove chicken when cooked—after an hour or so on a low flame—and use it for a fricassee, chicken salad, etc.

To boiling chicken stock, add a few pieces of left-over chicken and any kind of small or broken-up egg noodles. Cook until noodles are soft, and serve warm.

Whatever is left can be put in a refrigerator container and used again. Be sure to boil the soup and let it cool before serving a second time.

Let it stew gently, until the chicken falls apart. Some use nutmeg. A little parsley, shredded fine, is an improvement. A few pieces of cracker may be thrown in.
—The American Frugal Housewife
Mrs. Child, 1829

Cheese Sticks

INGREDIENTS
1 lb. sharp cheese, grated
1¼ lb. butter
1 egg
1 tbs. cold water
1⅓ cups flour
½ tsp. salt
paprika

TO MAKE

The butter and cheese should be at room temperature. Cream them together. Add the egg and the water, and beat well. Add the flour and salt, stirring between siftings. If it is a hot day, chill the dough for an hour. Otherwise, take about ⅓ of the dough and roll it out between two pieces of wax paper. Remove one piece of wax paper and turn the dough onto a buttered cookie sheet. Then remove the second piece of wax paper. With a knife, slice the dough into 3″ or so strips. Sprinkle with paprika.

Cook in a medium oven (350–375°) until light brown, about 15 minutes. When done, take them off the cookie sheet and score again, to separate the pieces. When cooled, put them in an air-tight container. This makes a big yield, and adults like them as well as children. They will go quickly.

—The Home and Its Management
Mabel Hyde Kittredge, 1917

Deviled Eggs

Some children will eat eggs. Many claim they detest them. Aside from using as many eggs as possible in cooking and baking recipes, you can fix deviled eggs for a child. They seem more appealing, and any left-overs will be eaten gladly by the adults.

INGREDIENTS

eggs
mustard
vinegar
worcestershire sauce
salt
celery salt
mayonnaise
paprika

TO MAKE

Before boiling the eggs, prick them at one end, then put them in cold water over a medium flame. Bring the water to a boil and let the eggs cook for about 15 minutes. Then drain, and cool with cold running water. When cold, peel the eggs, cut them in half, and remove the yolks.

In a small bowl, mash the egg yolks well. For six egg yolks, add a teaspoon of mustard, 1½ teaspoons of vinegar, 2 or 3 drops of worcestershire, a generous pinch of salt and a few shakes of celery salt. Start adding mayonnaise a little at a time. Keep mixing and adding mayonnaise until the mixture seems creamy. Fill the hard egg whites with the yolk mixture. For color and interest, shake paprika on top.

N.B.: The name "deviled" may bother a child. Whether or not you believe in the devil or hell, that is where the name comes from. To "devil" an egg means to heat it and to add strong seasonings.

Muffins

Muffins may not be the most nutritious type of snack food, but the home-made kind spread with honey and served with milk at a child's teatime are more wholesome than white bread and jelly. They can also be served to the whole family at breakfast or dinner. Besides, they are free of preservatives and make the kitchen smell good.

INGREDIENTS

1 egg, well beaten
2 cups sifted flour
1 cup milk
3 tbs. melted shortening
3 tsp. baking powder
3 tsp. sugar
½ tsp. salt

TO MAKE

Sift dry ingredients (flour, baking powder, sugar, salt) into a bowl. In a small separate bowl, mix milk, shortening and egg. Add the latter to the dry mixture. Stir just until all is moistened.

Drop by spoonfuls into greased muffin pans (each cup about two-thirds full). Cook in a 350° oven until light brown.

Sewing Society Nut Bread

INGREDIENTS

¾ cup sugar
2 eggs
1½ cups milk (approx.)
4 cups flour
4 tsp. baking powder
pinch of salt
¼ lb. nuts chopped fine
½ cup wheat germ—optional

TO MAKE

Pour the sugar into a large bowl. In a cup, beat the eggs and fill the cup with milk. Add to the sugar. Then add another cup of milk. Add the flour, sifted with the baking powder. Add salt and nuts and stir well.

Let stand in loaf pan 20 minutes. Bake at 350° for 45 minutes—but do not open the oven for the first 30 minutes.

My mother wrote down this recipe for me. It must date from about 1910.

Mama often made this bread to contribute to the Presbyterian Church Sewing Society suppers held every two weeks on Friday during the winter. After the afternoon sewing in the chapel, families came in for supper. The charge was 25¢ for adults, 10¢ for children.

—Edith Hopkins Hover

Oatmeal Cookies

INGREDIENTS

½ cup soft butter or shortening
1 cup brown sugar
2 eggs
2 cups flour
1 tsp. cinnamon
¼ tsp. salt
1 tsp. baking soda
2 cups uncooked oatmeal
¼ cup milk
1 tsp. vanilla
1 cup raisins and chopped nuts (optional)

TO MAKE

Mix butter and sugar in large bowl. Add eggs (beaten slightly). Sift in the flour with the cinnamon and salt. Mix the soda in 1 tablespoon water and add. Stir in oats, milk and vanilla. Add raisins and nuts. It should be a thick mixture.

In your hands, roll a teaspoon or so of the dough for each cookie and drop onto a greased cookie sheet. Bake 10 minutes at 375°. Cool and store in cookie tin.

Note: If the mixture seems too dry, add an extra egg. If the first pan of cookies spreads out too much and the cookies don't stay rounded, add one or more tablespoons of flour.

Nonsense Cookery

CRUMBOBBLIOUS CUTLETS

Procure some strips of beef. When the whole is minced, brush it up hastily with a new clothes-brush. Stir round rapidly and capriciously with a salt-spoon or a soup-ladle.

Place the whole in a saucepan, and remove it to a sunny place,—say the roof of the house if free of sparrows or other birds,—and leave it there for about a week.

Then add a little lavender, some oil of almonds, and a few herring-bones. Cover the whole with 4 gallons of clarified crumbobblious sauce.

Cut it into the shape of ordinary cutlets, and serve it in a clean tablecloth or dinner-napkin.

—Edward Lear, 1812–1888

Granola Mix

INGREDIENTS

6 cups uncooked oatmeal
½ cup brown sugar
¾ cup wheat germ—optional
½ cup shredded or flaked coconut
½ cup sesame seeds
1 cup chopped walnuts, pecans, peanuts or unchopped raisins
½ cup cooking oil
⅓ cup honey or ½ cup blackstrap molasses
1½ tsp. vanilla

TO MAKE

Heat oats in shallow pan in 325° oven for 10 minutes. In a large bowl, combine dry ingredients with heated oats. Add oil, honey and vanilla to the mixture.

Grease two wide oven pans. Divide the mixture between them and spread thin. Cook for 20 minutes, stirring and then spreading every 5 minutes. Cool. Crumble and store in jars in refrigerator.

Nothing could be healthier for children. Pour some in a dish, and let them eat it with their fingers. A cup of this mixture can also be added to any basic sugar cookie recipe.

Homemade Crackers

INGREDIENTS

3 eggs
2 cups flour
1 tsp. salt
1 tbs. butter
1 tbs. shortening
½ cup milk

TO MAKE

Mix all ingredients thoroughly. If mixture seems sticky, add flour. If it seems dry, add milk. Take a third of the dough at a time and roll it out as thin as possible (dough will be stiff). Cut in small rounds and bake on buttered cookie sheet, at 350°, for 20 minutes or until light brown.

Yield: approximately three dozen textury soda crackers. For children, serve plain or with cheese or peanut butter. To make the crackers more healthful, try different kinds of darker flour and add wheat germ. Just take care the dough is not too heavy. These crackers can also be appreciated by adults at teatime or as an hors d'oeuvre before dinner.

Bread Pudding

INGREDIENTS

1 cup bread crumbs
2 cups milk
1 egg
½ tsp. salt
3 tbs. sugar

TO MAKE

Soak the bread crumbs (they can be stale, or saved-up end pieces) in the milk. In a smaller dish, beat the egg with the sugar and salt, and add to the bread mixture. Pour all into a buttered baking dish and bake at a medium temperature for 30 or 40 minutes. The pudding is done when you can insert a knife and have it come out clean.

Serve with milk and a little extra sugar.

Keep a supply of stale bread crumbs on hand, ready to use at any time.

—Putnam's Household Handbook
Mae Savell Croy, 1916

Moravian Sugar Cake

This coffee cake was my personal Sunday-morning childhood joy. It dates from the time of the First World War, when my mother's family was determined to save "vital" food supplies. I have enriched the recipe.

INGREDIENTS

2 eggs
1 cup sugar
2 cups flour
pinch of salt
2 tsp. baking powder
1 cup milk
raisins
butter
cinnamon
brown sugar

TO MAKE

In a large bowl, mix the sugar, one cup flour, the eggs and the salt. Then add the milk, a little at a time. Sift the second cup of flour with the baking powder. Give it about three siftings, and in between, throw in a handful of raisins. That way the raisins are flour-coated and will not stick together or sink to the bottom.

Spread this out in a glass or metal baking container, about 9" x 9". Put a dozen or so lumps of butter on the top, sprinkle with cinnamon, and cover thickly with dark brown sugar. Bake for about a half-hour in a 350° oven. Do not overcook or the edges will become hard.

Date Balls

INGREDIENTS

1 lb. dates
1 cup sugar
1 egg
¼ lb. butter
2 cups Rice Krispies
1 cup pecans
wheat germ—optional

TO MAKE

Chop the dates slightly. In a pan, mix them with the sugar, the egg and the butter. Simmer to the gooey stage. In a bowl, pour the mixture over the cereal mixed with ½ cup wheat germ, plus the pecans, chopped finely. Form into small balls and roll in sugar (superfine sugar works well, but I prefer natural sugar).

Dates are very healthy food, and this recipe may be one way of getting your child used to the taste. The result is also special enough to use for adult party desserts—or it can be saved for everyone until Christmas.

Top-of-the-Stove Custard

One Serving

INGREDIENTS

one egg
one tsp. sugar
milk

TO MAKE

Break an egg in a custard cup. Add sugar and mix. Fill the cup with milk and stir. Place in a shallow pan with water well below the top of the cup. Boil for ten minutes. Allow to cool.

Cooks generally think it needless, when only one or two eggs are to be used, to beat them. It is an error: eggs injure everything unless they are made light before they are used.
—The Virginia Housewife
Mrs. Mary Randolph, 1860

Oven Custard

INGREDIENTS
4 eggs
⅓ cup sugar
2 cups milk
pinch of salt
vanilla, a few drops

TO MAKE

Beat all by hand, or mix in blender briefly. Fill custard cups two-thirds full. Heat oven to 350° and, when hot, insert shallow oven pan half full of water. Then place custard cups in pan and cook until slightly brown on top. Remove, cool and refrigerate.

Warning: carrying a pan full of water and custard cups to the oven is a difficult feat. I recommend two stages instead of one.

Compote of Stewed Fruit

Stewed fruit used to be a staple for children, usually served cold at breakfast. Fresh fruit is healthier, but a child who has trouble with fresh fruit may take to the slightly sweetened taste of cooked fruit.

Most any fruit can be stewed—apples, plums, peaches, raspberries, strawberries, pineapple. Just wash, peel, core, slice, remove seeds or whatever, and cook the fruit with a little sugar and water until it is soft. Cool and serve.

INGREDIENTS
1 cup prunes
2 tbs. raisins
1 sliced orange

1 sliced lemon
1 cup water
1 tbs. sugar

TO MAKE

Place all fruit in a double boiler with water and sugar. Simmer until fruit is tender. If necessary, add more sugar after cooking.

Fruits are an ideal food. Some contain 70% of the purest kind of distilled water in Nature's laboratory, ready for immediate absorption into the blood. Also, the starch of the fruit has, by the sun's action, been converted into glucose and is practically ready for assimilation.
—The Royal Road to Health
Charles A. Tyrrell, M.D., 1908

Ices on Sticks

There are plastic molds sold commercially now for popsicles made at home, but there is another way. Fill small, bathroom-size paper cups with lemonade, orangeade, a healthy fruit drink of any kind, sherbet or yogurt. Popsicle sticks can be bought inexpensively in dime stores. Put one stick in each cup and leave the cups in the freezer until hard.

Smaller children will need help taking the cup off. They tend to pull and end up with just the stick. Put your hands around the cup for a moment, to warm the edges and loosen the popsicle. Or put it briefly under warm running water. Then the popsicle should come out by itself.

Tarts

This is an old Swedish recipe—and a total luxury for a child.

INGREDIENTS
¼ lb. butter, soft
1 cup flour
½ cup sugar
vanilla
almond paste or jam filling

TO MAKE

For the dough, combine the butter, flour, sugar and a few drops of vanilla. Squeezing it with your hands is the easiest, fastest way. Butter enough muffin pans to make about ten tarts. Put a spoonful of dough into each section and press it down with your fingers to make a half-inch thick cup. Save a little dough for the tops.

Fill each tart with either the almond paste or a jam that is not too sweet, such as gooseberry. With your hands, take a small piece of dough and roll it long enough to reach across the tart. Place two of these on each, crisscross. Bake in a 350° oven for about 20 minutes.

Aside from baking time, these tarts take only 20 minutes to prepare.

REMEDIES FOR COMMON AILMENTS IN CHILDREN

FEVER

Aside from whatever medicines you are giving the child, sponge him off every hour or two (oftener when fevers are higher) with diluted rubbing alcohol. In a small pan, mix one part alcohol to four parts water. The mixture is soothing, cleansing and helps reduce the fever.

Massaging down the back, in long slow strokes, will relieve the congestion of the brain.

—The Mothercraft Manual
Mary L. Read, 1916

CUTS

Rubbing alcohol is a good antiseptic. Clean the cut with soap and water. Then use alcohol on cotton to dab around the edges. (It will hurt if applied directly on the cut.) Then bandage.

MOSQUITO BITES

Rubbing alcohol reduces the itch.

DRY SKIN AND CHAPPED LIPS

Vaseline is as good as any expensive skin lotion. Cocoa butter also is inexpensive and free of chemicals, and most drugstores carry it. Keep it refrigerated and let it reach room temperature before using. Rub either thoroughly into the child's skin and then wipe off excess lightly with a soft cloth.

STYES, PINK EYE, TIRED EYES

Mix one teaspoon powdered borax (sodium borate) with one pint boiling water. Let it cool and pour into a sterile jar. Wash the eye(s) with cotton dipped into the mixture, but be sure not to dip twice with the same piece of cotton. Kept covered, the eyewash will last several days.

The action of many remedies is not entirely clear. If the selection is merely a matter of fashion, it is well to take into consideration the degree of toxicity and the price.

—The Diseases of Children
Dr. M. Pfaundler and Dr. A. Schlossmann, 1908

BEE STINGS

Put apple vinegar on the sting, then baking soda on top. Vinegar is a natural base mixture which counteracts the acid in the sting.

N.B.: In general, vinegar softens, purifies and cuts down the harmful mineral content in water. Used as a hair-washing rinse (about three tablespoons to a quart of water), it keeps a child's hair healthy and soft.

STOMACH ACHE

This can often be gas in the intestines or the lack of a bowel movement. It can also be the beginnings of a more serious problem. Try waiting it out a couple of hours with an at-home remedy.

–Warm water can be magic. To make it appealing, put about five drops of essence of peppermint into half a cup of warm water. The essence can be bought or ordered by the ounce from most drug or natural food stores.

–A cup of camomile tea is calming. Add honey as a sweetener. In teabags or loose form, camomile tea too can be found in drug and natural food stores.

–A hot water bag held to the stomach is comforting. Most young children will not stay still long enough for it to be useful, but keep trying.

RASHES

A soda bath is soothing for various skin ailments, from diaper rash to chicken pox to hives. Sprinkle a cup or so of bicarbonate of soda into the bath water. For a non-tub sponge bath, add one tablespoon of soda to one gallon of warm water.

Medicated baths are of much service in childhood.
　　　　　　　　—The Diseases of Infants and Children
　　　　　　　　J. P. Crozer Griffith, M.D., 1919

COUGH

The oldest remedy of all is honey and lemon, and it can help. If the cough is serious and the pediatrician has prescribed medicine, honey and lemon can be given in between the dosage hours without interfering with the prescription.

Put four or five tablespoons of honey into a small saucepan. Add the juice of a lemon. Heat until the two are well blended. When cool, give a teaspoon at a time.

The Child's House

HOUSEHOLD

If a woman feels within herself the ability to do every kind of housework with her own hands, it will give her a consciousness of power. When facing a task of which one is not the master, there is a feeling of confusion.

. . . A good receptacle for soiled clothes is a pickle barrel, price fifty cents.

—The Home and Its Management
Mabel Hyde Kittredge, 1917

I can't claim to have known the systematized, seasonal householding of the 1900 era, but I am convinced there were many efficient women who maintained a calm schedule in their homes. Mama did the wash on Monday and ironed on Tuesday. Live-in Aunt Allie did the baking on Wednesday. Papa practiced his tuba on Friday evening; Saturday night everybody took a bath.

In the early spring Mama walked with the children in the woods and found one frail patch of trailing arbutus. On April Fool's Day Papa ran to the window and shouted to the children, "Come look, the circus is coming into town!" Every year, the children believed him.

Life then was not all garden asparagus and fresh bed linen. Many families didn't have enough money to do anything but work hard and constantly. Children often got little attention. And some mothers weren't excellent organizers. My grandmother ignored her "duties" when she could. She was a baseball fiend and would let a summer afternoon's plans slide by completely while she glued herself to the radio to listen to a Babe Ruth game.

Still, many turn-of-the-century children could count on certain events, certain days, safe routines, and the certainness made their lives secure. We still have that rhythmical instinct, but the times are working against us. Our children play in a jungly vacant lot across the street: one morning the bulldozers are there clearing the land for a new house. A family settles into a house in a suburb of Cleveland: one day Daddy's company decides to transfer him to Minneapolis, and suddenly the family is packed into cartons labeled Elm Street, Somewhere.

Americans have always been a people on the move, but now is an unprecedented time of change—often not by personal choice. Families can adapt to change, but mothers have to know how to keep the home routine going. No matter where home is, they must hold on to their unique sets of domestic rituals. A mother who knows what she is doing, and when she is going to do it, reassures herself and all her family.

Change doesn't have to be geographical. It can be a mother going back to work, and a young child being thrust into a day-care center. The mother will have fewer hours at home, but her established pattern can still hold up. Even in the case of a marriage breaking up, a mother's regular system will help carry her and her children through the lonely transition.

Every family's pattern is different. No magic bulletin-board list will work universally. The material in this chapter is not meant to dictate but to prod mothers into thinking about their home systems. It covers everything from washing out milk stains to making a child's room special, and the ideas are old. Remembering old, quiet householding ways may help us into quiet patterns of our own.

Much household work is just routine, the more quickly done, the better. If you have the patience to let a child vacuum, good. Teach him how to put the powder in the clothes washer; but don't feel you have to do it every time.

Many ideas in this chapter are for the late afternoon, when a child grows restless and pines for his mother's attention. Instead of avoiding the child or getting down on all fours to play "doggie," a mother can explain that she is making him something: a pillow, a doll dress, a blanket. It may take only a half hour, but it will soothe the child and draw him into playing nearby, by himself, knowing that his mother cares. However, no mother should feel she has to work late into the night to finish the promised product.

A regular home schedule is healthy, but it can't and doesn't have to be perfect.

The loving handwork gestures from mother to child are constructive and help a woman's sense of inner peace. For a mother to feel content with herself is the main goal, because a mother at peace is a Pied Piper.

THINGS TO MAKE

Washcloths

MATERIALS
an old towel
scissors
needle and thread

TO MAKE

Mothers always need extra washcloths to quick-scrub children's faces and hands. When you have a bath towel that is growing thin, cut the strongest sections into squares of 10 inches or so. Turn the edges under twice and hem with a small stitch.

Use these throwaways also to teach a child to wash himself. Sew a loop made of ribbon, material or string (braided string holds well) to one corner and hang the washcloth on a peg or low hook in the bathroom. When the child is sure of what's his, he will feel better about washing or drying by himself.

Child's Work Apron

MATERIALS
oilcloth (approx. ½ yd.)
cloth cord and/or ribbon (approx. 1 yd.)
pencil
pinking shears
needle, thread and scissors

TO MAKE

Oilcloth in various colors and patterns can be bought at most dime stores or hardware stores. Half a yard should be enough for a work apron large enough to go two-thirds of the way around a child's hips and reaching no lower than his knees.

Draw the pattern on the back of the oilcloth. Cut with pinking shears so the material will not shred at the edges. Attach cording or ribbon at the neck, making a loop big enough that the child can slip the apron over his head by himself. Then sew two lengths of cord at the waist, long enough to tie in a bow at the back.

Any number of oilcloth pockets can be added, for tools, crayons, etc.

This apron costs practically nothing. The workmanship doesn't matter. It lasts well and needs nothing but sponge cleaning.

A child should on all ordinary occasions be as untrammeled by clothes as a puppy is untrammeled by his coat.
—Home, School and Vacation
Annie Winsor Allen, 1907

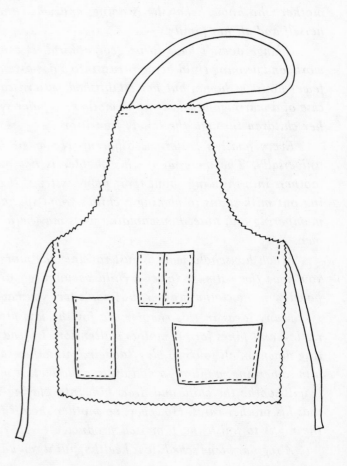

Embroidery on Children's Clothes

MATERIALS

a plain piece of child's clothing
cotton embroidery thread
large needle
a design, preplanned or free form

TO MAKE

Mothers used to enjoy embroidering baby clothes, necklines of toddlers' shirts, the bottoms of little girls' slips, and the like. They knew an impressive number of stitches, as some mothers still do. But embroidery doesn't have to be complicated. One timeless stitch, the chain stitch, will work for any line or outline design.

Insert the needle a short way from where you want to start, keeping the loose end on top (no knot). When you are finished, pull the end under with a small crochet hook and secure it by pulling it through a few nearby stitches. This way the stitches stay looser, and the free end doesn't get in your way, unseen, underneath the material.

Working from right to left (Figure A), insert the

Figure A. Chain Stitch

needle and bring it up where you plan to begin. Make a short stitch. The needle is under the material. Bring it back up through the thread in the middle of the first stitch. Make another short stitch and return the needle through the stitch before it. Keep doing this as evenly as you can and you will have delicate, clear designs. The sample designs (Figure B) are just sug-

Figure B. Sample Designs

gestions of what you can do with a chain stitch.

Any child will enjoy his mother's effort (and it can be very brief) to make his clothes special.

Flannel Sacque

Traditionally, these were made to protect babies from draughts. However, they can be made in any size—small for a doll—or larger for a little girl. They are comforting as bed jackets if children are sick.

Ask the child to stretch out her arms and measure from one wrist to the other. Cut out a perfectly round piece of flannel (or other washable, comfortable material) to that measurement, leaving a ½" at each edge for hemming. For a baby or a large doll, this might be 15". Pin the piece exactly in half and cut out a small semi-circle for the neck (again leaving room for hemming), a slit at each edge about a third of the way down (for arms), and make a cut up the front of the material to the neck edge. Unpin and hem all around, except for the arm slits (Figure A).

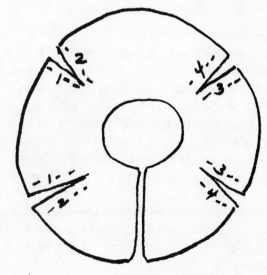

Figure A

With the material inside out, sew together #1 and #1, #2 and #2, #3 and #3, #4 and #4. Turn right side out (Figure B).

Figure B

To make the jacket fancy, you can bind the edges with ribbon and sew ribbon lengths at the neck for a bow, or embroider a simple flower at the top or a running stitch down the front.

—The Home and Its Management
Mabel Hyde Kittredge, 1917

Doll Dress

MATERIALS
a piece of cloth
scissors
needle and thread
yarn, snaps, or hooks and eyes—optional

TO MAKE
Cut a generous width of material so that it will go around the doll easily. Make the dress as long as you want, but leave space for hemming at both ends.

Fold the material in half twice, lengthwise. Estimate where the doll's arms will go and cut out a moon-shaped piece (Figure A). Unfold. Hem bottom and top. With a few running stitches, draw the top together with heavy thread, or yarn (Figure B) and tie at back.

To make it easier for the child who cannot yet tie a bow, secure the gathering and sew a snap or hook and eye at the top, or sew several down the back of the dress.

Vary this design at will. If you make more than

Figure A   Figure B

one, use plain cotton for everyday dresses and silk for parties. Sew on sequins or lace, add a ribbon sash—whatever occurs to you.

Common Linen Doll

MATERIALS
a piece of linen, thick muslin or other sturdy material
dress material (traditionally gingham or calico)
needle and threads to match the materials

TO MAKE
For the body, fold an 18″ square piece of linen in half, then roll it up lengthwise as tightly as possible. Pin half way down material so it will not unroll. For the head, gather the top outside edge with strong thread, pull tightly and secure at center. For the body, sew the roll one-third down the back of the doll, to the waist. Spread out the bottom part of the linen so that the doll will stand.

For the dress, cut a rectangle wide enough to go around the bottom of the linen easily. The length should cover the doll from the neck down. Gather at the top, leaving space for a small neck ruffle (not shown) if you like. Fasten the dress to the body with a few stitches. Tie a ribbon or string tightly around the waist. The back of the skirt should overlap so that sewing is not necessary. Hem the bottom of the skirt.

For the arms, roll up two small pieces of linen, sew them up the long side and at one end, neatly, for the hands. Cut small pieces of the dress material for sleeves, shirr them at one end and attach to the arms. Then sew the arms to the doll, just at the top of the frock.

These dolls answer every purpose for very small children. They may be made of any size, from 9" down to a finger's length. You may make a whole family, mother, children and babies.

—American Girl's Book
Miss Leslie, 1838

Child's Pillow

A child will be very happy if you make him his own pillow, for car trips, naps or just to carry around. He can use his old baby pillow, but the store-bought variety often is not washable and needs ironed pillow cases. One made with the materials below can be washed by hand in light suds. He may call it his "cool pillow," a child's description of something comforting and smooth to his face.

MATERIALS
*dark satin material
shredded foam rubber or old cut-up nylons
needle and heavy thread color to match material
light cotton material for inner pillow case—optional*

TO MAKE
If you wish, sew up an inner cotton covering, leaving the fourth side open. Otherwise, just start with the satin. A heavy, brocaded piece works well. Often a thrift shop or remnant piece can be found. Put right sides together and sew around three edges. Then turn the material right side out, insert the foam rubber (not

too full) and sew up the remaining side.

Before stuffing the pillow, you can decorate it with the child's initials or with a pre-embroidered flower or animal patch. This can also be an inexpensive and not very time-consuming birthday present for friends' children.

Child's Blanket

It is a pleasure to make a child his very own blanket. As with pillows, the child may cling to his original baby blankets, but as he grows, he needs something larger to crawl under. His extra joy is that you made it especially for him.

MATERIALS
*a 4- or 5-foot length of pre-quilted cotton batting
equal length of cotton print, dark satin, or other fabric
needle and heavy thread
yarn needle and washable yarn to match top material*

TO MAKE
Quilted cotton batting can be bought in different widths. One side is a smooth quilted surface. The other is cottony. The material is inexpensive, but be sure it is a washable variety. Just as in making a pillow, lay the pieces face to face and pin around the edges. Stretch and pin carefully so there will be no sags or bumps when you are finished. Sew three sides, an inch or two in from the edge. Turn right side out, and fold in and pin the last side. Sew it shut, preferably using a blanket stitch.

To make sure the blanket can go through repeated machine washings, fasten it in various places (geometrically or haphazard) with yarn. With a threaded yarn needle, sew down from the top and pull up from the bottom, close to the first stitch. Cut the ends allowing 2 inches or so, and double-tie the pieces of yarn together.

This is a simplified version of a patchwork quilt. A simpler sort is made from a worn cotton blanket, cut to size and hemmed as necessary. To make it special, buy good quality ribbon and, at one end, sew on the child's first name in big block letters. As an added pleasure for the child, buy wide satin ribbon and sew it onto the top edge of the blanket.

ACCUMULATED SUGGESTIONS

BULLETIN BOARD

Good in the kitchen, preferably above the kitchen table. For a child it can be a living scrapbook: silly or pretty magazine pictures, his latest drawing, postcards or photographs. It is also an effortless way to help the child into letters, numbers, art, history or any subject you choose. A writing pad and a pencil on a string give the mother a place for notes and shopping lists. Watching a mother write encourages a child to make his own "lists."

KITCHEN TABLE

In a crowded kitchen, a small table attached to the wall by hinges, with a support underneath which reaches the floor (also hinged so that it will fold flat when not in use), is a great help. It can be a breakfast or lunch table, an ironing surface or an extra cooking space, and folded away when not needed. A dining table may be made the same way, only it must be fastened more securely to the wall.

—The American Farm and Home Cyclopædia, *1887*

WINTER PARAPHERNALIA
Hooks at a low level teach children how and where to hang up coats, jackets, etc. Sew a cloth loop in the back of each coat to make hanging up easier. A box or basket underneath the coat hooks can be used for hats and mittens.

DECORATING CHILDREN'S ROOMS
Always keep an eye out for fabric remnants in department stores and notion or thrift shops. If you find a piece that's big enough, make a bedspread, hemming all the edges. If you sew four folded-over, fitted corners, it will be like a contour sheet. When the child plays and jumps on the bed, the cover will not be constantly on the floor. Use smaller fabric pieces for a ruffle at the bottom of the bed, or for curtains (half or whole), or just for a ruffle at the top of the window.

Do not furnish the child's room with any old pieces, taking it for granted that he is too young to care. The room should be pleasing to the child.
> —The Home and Its Management
> *Mabel Hyde Kittredge, 1917*

PILLOWS
Any plain pillow case can be dressed up with a lace edge, appliques or crewel or embroidered designs. Children love any effort you put into their sleeping pillows. If the pillow is pretty, leave it on top of the bedspread, as part of the room design.

When one considers the comfort of having a handsome set of pillow shams, the outlay of time does not appear to have been wasted.
> —The American Farm and Home Cyclopædia, 1887

STAINS
Milk: Wash out as quickly as possible in warm water, using a pure soap rather than detergent.
Coffee and Fruit: If the material is large (especially tablecloths), drape the stained part over a large bowl. Pour boiling water on it. Pour from a height to give the water force. With smaller pieces, put them in a large pot of boiling water for twenty minutes or so, and stir frequently.
Blood: Wash quickly in cold water. If the stain remains, scrub with soap and soak in warm water.
Chewing Gum: Pull it off with ice.
Grass: Wash out the stain with a basic yellow soap (Borax puts one out). Then put the clothes in the washer. Soaking the stain with buttermilk also works.

N.B.: Yellow soap also makes a good wash for children who have been playing near poison ivy.

Boiling water removes coffee spots; cold water removes cocoa spots, and sunshine removes many spots.
> —Putnam's Household Handbook
> *Mae Savell Croy, 1916*

FRESH FLOWERS AND CUT GREENS
Add a few small pieces of charcoal to the water, and the vaseful will last longer. Ideally, the water should be changed each day. Also, anything bought at a flower shop should be cut at the end with a razor on a sharp diagonal.

DRY ROOM AIR
Put a pitcher or bowl of cold water—the colder the better—in the room. The water absorbs stale gases and increases the humidity. It should be changed every few days.

STICKING DRAWERS OR DOORS
Rub the slides or edges with soap.

SPONGES
To keep them fresh, rub with lemon and rinse in warm water. Also, they can be washed in the clothes washer.

IRONING BOARD PAD
Fold up an old blanket and lay it on the board. Cover the blanket with a sheet, double thickness, and pin the sheet under the board. You need never buy a commercial ironing board cover.

CLEANING MARBLE
To remove serious stains, rub gently with a pumice stone. Lemon juice will take off lighter marks. For general cleaning, use soap and water, but be sure to rinse well. A plain oil, like linseed or lemon oil, helps marble keep its shine.

WINDOW CLEANING
Add vinegar to water—about 2 tablespoons to one quart water. This leaves less film than commercial products. Put it in a spray bottle to make life easier.

Wipe the glass with sheets of newspaper—they absorb well and cost nothing.

BURNED PANS

Aluminum—immerse the pan right away in a larger pan of cold water. Soak, and scrub later. For sticky pans of any kind, put in a few drops of ammonia, fill with water and leave overnight. Wash the next day. For general pan stains that will not scrub off, cook some fresh beets in the pan and then try cleaning again. Have the fresh-cooked beets for supper.

OVEN CLEANING

Instead of the powerful, dangerous modern cleaners, try ammonia. Put ½ cup ammonia in a not valuable china cup and leave it in the oven overnight, door closed. Next day, dilute the ammonia with water in a bucket, put on rubber gloves, and use the mixture to wash the oven.

REFRIGERATOR CLEANING

Baking soda with water cleans well and leaves no chemical residue. The inside of the refrigerator will smell fresh.

STEAM IRONS

(Admittedly this is not a suggestion from the past, when there were no steam irons, but it is so useful that I have taken the liberty of including it.) Use distilled water. Tap water is full of minerals that leave a deposit which eventually clogs the steam holes. The melted ice from a defrosted freezer can be used in an iron; it is mineral-free. If the steam holes become encrusted, break up the deposit with a heavy needle. Then rub the bottom of the iron with fine steel wool. To make the bottom really smooth, run the iron (warm) over a piece of paraffin wrapped in a towel set aside for that purpose.

SOAP

Buy in quantity and save money. If the soap is perfumed, store it in the linen closet as a sachet. Also, soap that has several months to dry out goes further. Save small pieces of soap. When you have five or six, wrap them together in a piece of cheesecloth and dunk them in a bowl of hot water. They will melt into each other to make a new cake of soap.

SWEET KITCHEN SMELL

Put a few whole cloves in a small pan of water and boil them for a few minutes.

LINEN CLOSET

Put newly laundered sheets and towels at the bottoms of their respective piles. With rotation, the linens will wear evenly. This system was mentioned in Napoleon's household staff routines.

MOTH BALLS

Moths lay their eggs in late May or early June, so cover your winter clothes before then. Save some old nylons to use as mothball bags. Fill the bags with half a dozen mothballs each and tie one up every few hangers. This way, the mothballs are easier to get rid of in the fall than if you have thrown them willy-nilly into the bottom of the bag or into the pockets of every wool coat.

WASHING WOOL

One way to make fewer trips to the dry cleaner is to wash wool. In fact, a clothes brush often makes a big improvement, or sponging off spots with a slightly soapy rag. Few women now have the clothesline space or energy to wash big wool blankets or winter coats, but smaller items can be cleaned at home. The night before you wash, dampen the wool with cool water and wrap in a sheet. This way it shrinks as little as possible. The next day, wash in cool water with pure soap—not detergent. Wool hats can be dried on an upside-down bowl that matches the original shape. Sweaters, dresses and the like have to be laid flat on towels and pushed or pulled to their correct size. When the wool is about two-thirds dry, steam-press it. New wool material for sewing should be washed this way before work is started.

SETTING COTTON COLORS

Different chemicals are used to dye each color in cotton material, so the following salt rinse can only be said to work with most cottons. Dissolve 1 cup of salt in one gallon of cold water. Soak the material in it for two hours, then rinse well in cold water. If the material is going to shrink, it will do so even in cold water. The salt has no effect on shrinkage.

Natural dyes have almost entirely disappeared. One exception is Cochineal, a dye extracted from the females of a species of bugs which grows on cactus plants. It is still used to color the red coat of the British soldier.

—Household Textiles
Charlotte M. Gibbs, 1912

HEM CREASES

When letting down dresses or pants, use white vinegar to get rid of the old hemline. In a saucer, dilute the vinegar slightly, sponge the back of the material, and iron.

TOOTH POWDER

For everyone in the family, baking soda once or twice a week will remove stains and tartar that regular toothpastes miss, and it is less expensive. From a box kept in the bathroom, just shake some on the toothbrush.

LAST SUGGESTION

In winter, always set the handle of your pump as high as possible.

—The American Frugal Housewife
Mrs. Child, 1836

The Child's Room

Inside a house, I would wish for every child: space, a few ways to exercise his body and his mind on a wide scale, pictures on the wall, and a minimum of small toys.

Lucky are the children who have an attic or basement room in which to let go. Luckier still are the children who can run outdoors at will. As for the city child, and the suburban child in winter, much of the time his physical freedom is only in his own room.

Ideally, a child's room or playroom should be spacious and basic. The illustration suggests a large family, but the ideas can be adapted for even a single child. A rocking horse is shown, plus an indoor seesaw, small chairs and a few oriental wall panels. Other old staples, not shown here, are a simple proscenium arch and platform for "shows," a small upright piano for children to pound on, a worktable and bench. There could also be a baby's corner (with playpen, bolted baby swing and so on) to help brothers and sisters of different ages know their own spaces and abilities.

A playroom which is fitted as a gymnasium with swing trapeze and monkey rope is altogether a particularly happy nursery.

—The House and Its Equipment
Laurence Weaver, 1912

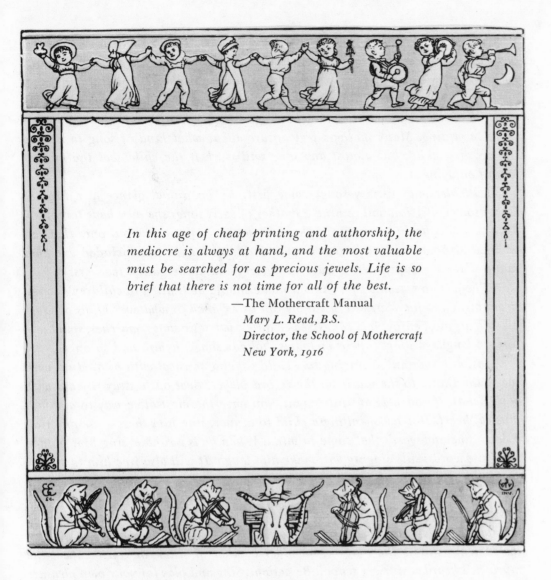

In this age of cheap printing and authorship, the mediocre is always at hand, and the most valuable must be searched for as precious jewels. Life is so brief that there is not time for all of the best.
—The Mothercraft Manual
Mary L. Read, B.S.
Director, the School of Mothercraft
New York, 1916

The Child's Spirit

MUSIC

Children, like birds, learn to sing by imitation, and it is not too early to start a child's musical education the day he is born, by singing to him.
—Creative Music for Children
Satis N. Coleman, 1922

After a child's immediate physical needs are cared for, music is a mother's first tool of love. For centuries women have known that lullabies and rocking are the most natural ways to soothe a baby. From a mother's singing, a baby learns the reassuring sound of her voice and the beginnings of what will be his native tongue.

Mothers sing less to babies now than in the past. They worry about picking a baby up too often, "spoiling" him with too much rocking, hugging and cooing. I think any practice that·comforts the baby, and the mother, is good; singing is an effective means.

When the infant reaches preschool age, singing is still important and even more rewarding. Many mothers feel unsure about what kind of song to sing to the growing child, but almost any song will work if the child sees the mother herself enjoying it.

Lullabies and nursery songs come first. An occasional glance at a Mother Goose song collection will remind a mother of early songs she may have forgotten. Two-year-olds begin to enjoy simple game songs. I offer a few old ones that can be used at home with only one or two children. I have not included any that require larger groups; these I leave to nursery and kindergarten teachers.

There is no reason why a child at home should be limited to children's songs. From birth and for years afterward, he can be exposed to whatever kinds of songs his parents most enjoy: folk songs, sea chanties, patriotic songs, marches, spirituals, foreign language songs, opera melodies, holiday songs, hymns and so on.

Just as important as singing to a child is being musical with him. Hum with the radio. Dance to the music on the record player. Beat out a stray rhythm with your hands. If you play an instrument, you have the most alive way to a child's musical heart. Instead of calling a child to dinner, sing him there—use any ridiculous tune and words that come to mind. When he is irritable, sing him sudden nonsense words; silly singing will make him laugh. It will also free him to answer you in his own made-up words and tunes.

It is important to start singing early, because a three- or four-year-old may ask you to stop. He may be hearing his own drummer and not want his music dictated. He may take to his own record player, try out his own small musical instruments, mimic the songs of an older brother or sister, or try to repeat the music he's heard at nursery school. Be patient. Sing and play for your own pleasure and let the child tag along as he wishes.

Children differ, but most young ones love songs improvised by their mothers. The lyrics may change, but the melody and subject can become a wonderful bedtime ritual. Use a familiar tune, or make one up. The words don't have to rhyme. Just sing about a favorite doll or stuffed animal, summer pastimes, the garbage collector or the hot-dog man. To give yourself time to think up the next verse, have a short chorus repeat for a crutch. For example:

Hot-dog man, hot-dog man, I would like ten hot dogs.
One is for my mother, and nine are just for me.

CHORUS
Hot-dog man, hot -dog man, outdoors all the time.
Winter or summer, outdoors rain or shine.

As the child grows, he will begin to give you suggestions for lyrics. Eventually, he will tire of the song game. This is sad for the willing mother, but she can be sure that the hours spent were not wasted. The more music a child absorbs at home, the more it will be a part of him forever.

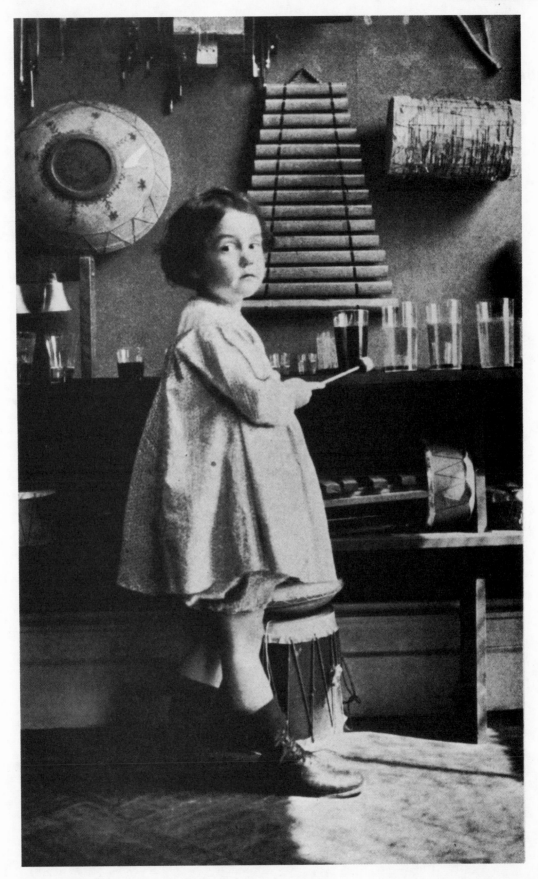

LULLABIES AND NURSERY SONGS

Hush, Little Baby

*Depending on who is singing use the word "Mama" or "Papa." This is a riddle song as
well as a lullaby and will make three and four-year-olds happy.*

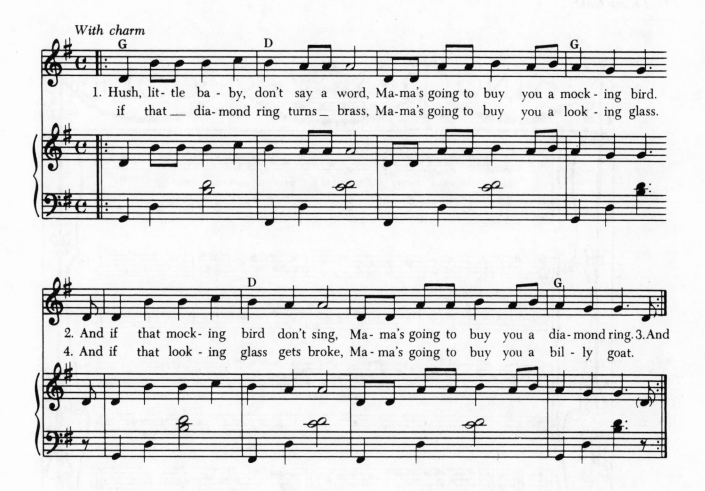

With charm

1. Hush, lit-tle ba-by, don't say a word, Ma-ma's going to buy you a mock-ing bird.
   if that __ dia-mond ring turns __ brass, Ma-ma's going to buy you a look-ing glass.

2. And if that mock-ing bird don't sing, Ma-ma's going to buy you a dia-mond ring. 3. And
4. And if that look-ing glass gets broke, Ma-ma's going to buy you a bil-ly goat.

5. If that billy goat won't pull,
   Mama's going to buy you a cart and bull.

6. If that cart and bull turn over,
   Mama's going to buy you a dog named Rover.

7. And if that dog named Rover won't bark,
   Mama's going to buy you a horse and cart.

8. And if that horse and cart fall down,
   You'll still be the sweetest little baby in town.

Old King Cole

Words from Mother Goose
Tune Traditional

Twinkle, Twinkle, Little Star

Moderato

1. Twin-kle, twin-kle, lit-tle star; How I won-der what you are,
2. When the blaz-ing sun is gone, When he noth-ing shines up-on,

Up a-bove the world so high, Like a dia-mond in the sky!
Then you show your lit-tle light, Twin-kle, twin-kle all the night.

Twin-kle, twin-kle lit-tle star, How I won-der what you are!

3. Then the trav'ller in the dark
   Thanks you for your tiny spark;
   He could not see which way to go,
   If you did not twinkle so.

4. In the dark blue sky you keep,
   While you thro' my window peep,
   And you never shut your eye,
   Till the sun is in the sky.

—Original Poems for Infant Minds
Ann and Jane Taylor, 1804

Evening Prayer

(Hansel and Gretel)

E. HUMPERDINCK

GAME SONGS

Edith F. Foster 87

Ring Around a Rosy

This is an ancient singing game known in America since the eighteenth century at least, and even earlier in Germany and France. "Rosy" is a hand-me-down from the French *rosier,* meaning rose tree.

As a game song, it can be used from the time the child first learns to walk, and for long afterward. Just hold hands with one or more children in a circle, dance around, and on "all fall down," collapse.

Old singing game

Words and tune traditional

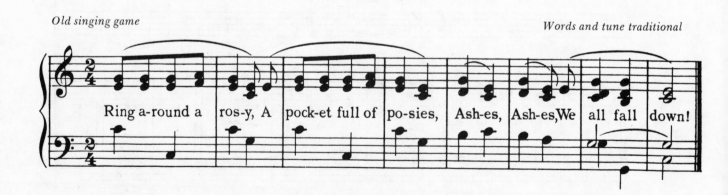

Ring a-round a ros-y, A pock-et full of po-sies, Ash-es, Ash-es, We all fall down!

Hokey Pokey

With a group of children, form a circle and have them follow the directions of the lyrics with the different parts of their bodies. To "Hokey Pokey" is just to wiggle your whole body. This game works even with a mother and only one or two children—and with a wide age range. Use whatever other parts of the body occur to you.

Bouncy

1. You put your right foot in, You put your right foot out,
2. You put your left foot in, You put your left foot out,

You put your right foot in And you shake it all a - bout,
You put your left foot in And you shake it all a - bout,

And then you do the ho - key - po - key, And you turn your - self a - bout,
And then you do the ho - key - po - key And you turn your - self a - bout,

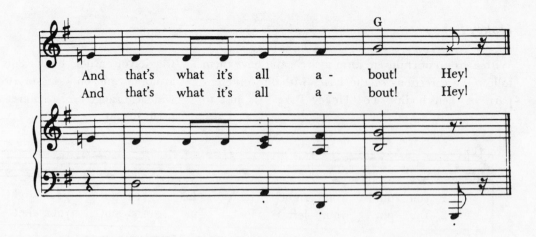

And that's what it's all a - bout! Hey!
And that's what it's all a - bout! Hey!

3. *You put your right elbow in, etc.*
4. *You put your left elbow in, etc.*
5. *You put your nose in, etc.*
6. *You put your stomach in, etc.*
7. *You put your whole self in, etc.*

This game was once danced deliberately and decorously, as old fashion dictated. Now it has been turned into a romp. The English name is "Hinkumbooby."

—Games and Songs of American Children
William Wells Newell, 1883

Skip to My Lou

If a mother and one or two children are playing, they hold hands and skip round and round .during the "Skip to my Lou" refrain, or take turns skipping around each other.

If there is a larger group of children, a circle game can be played. One child stands in the center of the circle. As the first verse begins, he chooses a partner to skip with him around the inside of the circle. After the verse and refrain, the first child goes back to the circle, and the second child chooses a new partner.

Lightly
Chorus

Lou, Lou, skip to my Lou, Lou, Lou, skip to my Lou,

MEASURE 7

Lou, Lou, skip to my Lou, Skip to my Lou, my dar - ling.

1. Lost my __ part - ner, what - 'll I ___ do? Lost my __ part - ner, what - 'll I ___ do?
2. I'll get an - oth - er one, pret - ti - er than you, I'll get an - oth - er one, pret - ti - er than you,

MEASURE 15

Lost my __ part - ner, what - 'll I ___ do? Skip to my Lou, my dar - ling.
I'll get an - oth - er one, pret - ti - er than you, Skip to my Lou, my dar - ling.

3. *Fly in the sugar bowl, shoo, fly, shoo, etc.*
4. *Rats in the bread tray. How they chew! etc.*
5. *Rabbit in the cornfield, big as a mule, etc.*
6. *Cow in the kitchen, moo, cow, moo, etc.*
7. *Hogs in the garden, rooting up food, etc.*

NONSENSE SONGS

Sing a Song of Sixpence

Pop! Goes the Weasel

Beginning as a seventeenth-century English children's song, the tune was later brought to America. The verses changed, and by the nineteenth century it had become a popular square dance melody.

Words and tune traditional

All a-round the cob-bler's bench, The mon-key chased the wea-sel, The mon-key thought 'twas all in fun, Pop! goes the wea-sel. A pen-ny for a spool of thread, A pen-ny for a nee-dle, That's the way the mon-ey goes, Pop! goes the wea-sel.

FOLK BALLAD

A Fox Went Out

3. He grabbed the grey goose by the neck,
   Threw a duck across his back,
   He didn't mind their "Quack, quack, quack,"
   And their legs all dangling down-o, down-o, down-o,
   He didn't mind their "Quack, quack, quack,"
   And their legs all dangling down-o.

4. He ran till he came to his own den,
   And there were his little ones, eight, nine, ten,
   They cried, "Daddy, you'd better go back again
   Cause it must be a mighty fine town-o, town-o, town-o,
   Daddy, you'd better go back again
   Cause it must be a mighty fine town-o."

5. The fox and his wife without any strife
   Cut up the goose with a fork and knife,
   They never had such a supper in their life
   And the little ones chewed on the bones-o,
   Bones-o, bones-o.
   Never had such a supper in their life
   And the little ones chewed on the bones-o.

MARCHES AND PATRIOTIC SONGS

Battle Hymn of the Republic

JULIA WARD HOWE

Glo - ry, Glo - ry, Hal - le - lu - jah! Glo - ry, Glo - ry, Hal - le -

lu - jah! His truth is march - ing on!

When Johnny Comes Marching Home Again

March tempo

L. LAMBERT

1. When John - ny comes march - ing home a - gain, Hur - rah! Hur -
2. The old church bell will peal with joy, Hur - rah! Hur -
3. Get read - y for the ju - bi - lee, Hur - rah! Hur -

rah! We'll give him a heart - y wel - come then, Hur -
rah! To wel - come home our dar - ling boy, Hur -
rah! We'll give the he - ro three times three, Hur -

rah! ____ Hur - rah! ____ The _ men will cheer, __ the
rah! ____ Hur - rah! ____ The _ vil - lage lads __ and
rah! ____ Hur - rah! ____ The _ lau - rel wreath _ is

boys will shout, The la - dies they _ will all turn out, And we'll
las - sies say, With ro - ses they _ will strew the way, And we'll
rea - dy now, To place up - on _ his loy - al brow,

all feel gay when John - ny comes march - ing home. __

Yankee Doodle

The "Yankee Doodle" melody is English and centuries old. In this country, lyrics were invented for it about the French and Indian War, Narragansett Bay clam boating, and the Civil War, but most especially the Revolutionary War.

Children laugh at the mere sound of the words "Yankee Doodle." *Yankee* is supposed to be a corruption of an Indian effort to say *English*. A *doodle* is a foolish simpleton. While willingly making fun of themselves and their often ragged appearance, the 1776 volunteer regiments sang "Yankee Doodle" and marched to victory.

Merrily

1. Fath'r and I went down to camp, A - long with Cap - tain Good - in', And

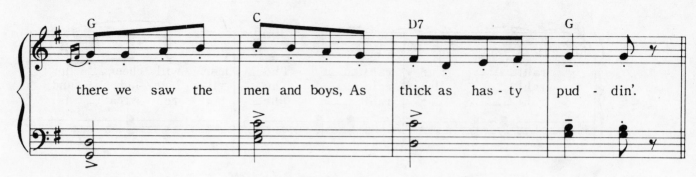

there we saw the men and boys, As thick as has-ty pud-din'.

Chorus

Yan - kee Doo-dle keep it up, Yan - kee Doo-dle Dan-dy,

Mind the mu-sic and the step, And with the girls be han-dy.

2. And there we saw a thousand men,
   As rich as Squire David;
   And what they wasted ev'ry day,
   I wish it could be saved.

   CHORUS

3. And there was Captain Washington
   Upon a slapping stallion,
   A-giving orders to his men;
   I guess there was a million.

   CHORUS

4. And then the feathers on his hat,
   They looked so 'tarnal fine, ah!
   I wanted peskily to get
   To give to my Jemima.

   CHORUS

5. But I can't tell the half I see,
   They kept up such a smother;
   So I took my hat off, made a bow,
   And scampered home to mother.

   CHORUS

Popular version

1. Oh, Yankee Doodle went to town,
   A-riding on a pony
   He stuck a feather in his crown
   And called it macaroni.

   CHORUS

2. First he bought a porridge pot,
   And then he bought a ladle,
   And then he trotted home again
   As fast as he was able.

   CHORUS

Dixie Land

DAN EMMET

Chorus

Land. Then — I wish I was in Dix - ie, Hoo - ray! Hoo ray! In — Dix - ie Land, I'll take my stand to live and die in Dix - ie. A - way, a - way, a - way down south in Dix - ie, A - way, a - way, a - way down south in Dix - ie!

2. *This world was made in just six days,*
   And finished up in various ways.
   Look away! Look away! Look away! Dixie Land.
   They then made Dixie trim and nice,
   And Adam called it "Paradise."
   Look away! Look away! Look away! Dixie Land.

   CHORUS

FRENCH CHILDREN'S SONG

Sur le Pont d'Avignon

Sur le Pont d'Avignon

The French nursery equivalent of "London Bridge," this song concerns a bridge built in the twelfth century over the Rhone River. In the Middle Ages, bridges were extremely important structures, the settings for markets, festivals, trials and even executions.

2. Les belles dames font comme ça *(girls curtsey)*
   Et puis encore comme ça.

3. Les musiciens font comme ça *(pretend to play violin, etc.)*
   Et puis encore comme ça.

4. Les militaires font comme ça *(children salute)*
   Et puis encore comme ça.

RYHMES AND MORE

Have in the house a good collection of children's verse.
What the child enjoys, he will ask to hear again. Give him
his favorites often. Soon the child will repeat parts of them
himself.

—Home, School and Vacation
Annie Winsor Allen, 1907

From birth, a child can be sung to. The mother's next love tool is the world of
rhymes. Rhymes are word rhythms without music, and a mother knows instinc-
tively when to talk happy rhymes.

Unfortunately, while instinct may prod a mother, it does not provide con-

69

crete material. Few young mothers now have the verse heritage that their mothers enjoyed. We have to teach ourselves the rhyme forms to use with a growing child.

Fingerplays come first. They are an old and warm tradition, but we use "Pat-a-Cake" and "This Little Pig Went to Market" over and over, for want of other touch-word plays. Children need to be touched, and fingerplays are one of the most natural ways to touch and love a child. Many delight a six-month-old and eventually help him begin to coordinate his fingers. In this chapter, I offer several well-worn examples which can be used all through the first years.

Also included are rhythmical children's prayers which can be started very early if parents wish to instill a religious belief in a child. The most widely used bedtime prayer is probably "Now I Lay Me Down to Sleep" (". . . If I should die before I wake . . ."). This seems to me a worrisome way to put a child to bed. I chose instead two old but more peaceful versions.

As a child grows, his rhyme world should grow with him. Parents can begin to use knee rides, Mother Goose verses, jingles and nonsense pieces. I emphasize old material here, but whether a mother is using old rhymes or new, she can put together her own scrapbook of favorites. The more she knows by heart, the better. However, having her own written collection close at hand makes it easier for her to use the world of rhymes.

After rhymes comes poetry, an intimidating word for many mothers. We would rather leave the whole subject alone until the child reaches school age. But poems come in all sizes, and you can start small. Poetry helps a child begin to treasure the careful choice of words. Good early verses have a reassuring Mother Goose singsong and also give the child more colorful and adventurous mental pictures than he has ever had before.

To begin, try reading with the child directly from poetry books. The illustrations will help hold his attention. Just read two or three short pieces at a time. If this system doesn't work, write out a single poem and tape it up in a prominent spot. Eventually the child will ask about it. Instead of answering, "It's a poem," tell him it's a funny story about a turtle or whatever. A child is more drawn to the word "story." Another way is to print the verses on sheets of cardboard, with illustrations (even stick figures) at the top. Number the big pages so that the child can turn them at the right time.

In all of this, take your lead from the child. When he begins to invent nonsense sentences, give him a jingle or a nonsense verse. When his attention span is obviously growing, try a longer poem. If it tires him, just stick to the first four lines and add more later. Look for a subject that you know excites the child, and length may suddenly be no problem at all.

Even when a child has grown into the poetry stage, he will have days when he needs to get back to a more babyish pace. Then a mother can reach back into her collection of fingerplays and rhymes that made the child laugh when he was younger. There is no law that says you cannot sometimes treat a five-year-old as a toddler, and rhymes are a wonderful way to be happy with a child who is struggling to find his inner rhythm.

FINGERPLAYS
AND KNEE RIDE

This game works from babyhood. The baby or child can be lying down, sitting in a chair or on the parent's lap.

Creep Mouse Creep

START SAYING:
Creep mouse, creep mouse,
creep mouse, creep mouse . . .
into baby's house.

Move creeping fingers slowly at first, then faster and faster, up the child's body, tickling the child's neck and then sliding fingers inside his shirt.

MOTHERCRAFT

Here's the Church

Here is the church (interlace fingers, with palms facing, fingers inside)
Here is the steeple (raise index fingers, tips touching to make a triangle)
Open the door (release thumbs as if opening door)
And out come the people (turn palms upward and wiggle fingers).

Knock at the Door

Knock at the door (*tap forehead*)
Peep in (*lift eyelid*)
Lift the latch (*tilt nose*)
Walk in (*put fingers inside child's mouth*)
Go way down cellar and eat apples. (*tickle under chin*)

Trot, Trot to Boston

In a lively singsong, with child (if small) on knee, or on mother's or father's lower leg for a wilder ride. Hold hands tight.
Trot, trot to Boston,
Trot, trot to Lynn,
Trot, trot home again,
And don't fall in. *(Down goes the child into the "ditch"—i.e., gently onto the floor)*

Here's a Ball for Baby

The mother holds the child on her lap, using his hands for the game. Or, she can sit in front of the child and have him imitate some of the gestures. For older children, use their names instead of saying "baby."

Here's a ball for baby, big and soft and round.
(thumbs and middle fingers make a circle)
Here's baby's hammer. Oh, how he can pound.
(pound one closed fist on top of other)
Here's baby's music, clapping, clapping so!
(hands clapping)
Here are baby's soldiers, standing in a row.
(hold up stiff fingers)
Here's baby's trumpet, toot-too-too-too!
(hands held at mouth, like a trumpet)
Here's the way baby plays at peek-a-boo.
(hands cover and uncover eyes)
Here's a big umbrella to keep baby dry.
(hold palm of one hand over upright index finger of other hand)
Here's baby's cradle, rock-a-baby-bye!
(fold arms and rock)

NONSENSE

If a Pig Wore a Wig

If a pig wore a wig,
    What could we say?
Treat him as a gentleman,
    And say "Good day."

If his tail chanced to fail,
    What could we do?—
Send him to the tailoress
    To get one new.

—Sing-Song
Christina Rossetti, 1872

Old Mother Hubbard and Her Dog

Old Mother Hubbard
Went to the cupboard,
  To get her poor Dog a bone:
But when she came there
The cupboard was bare
  And so the poor Dog had none.

She went to the baker's
  To buy him some bread,
But when she came back
  The poor Dog was dead.

She went to the joiner's
  To buy him a coffin,
But when she came back
  The poor Dog was laughing.

She took a clean dish
  To get him some tripe,
And when she came back
  He was smoking a pipe.

She went to the alehouse
  To get him some beer,
But when she came back
  The Dog sat in a chair.

She went to the tavern
  For white wine and red,
But when she came back
  The Dog stood on his head.

She went to the fruiterer's
  To buy him some fruit,
But when she came back
  He was playing the flute.

She went to the tailor's
  To buy him a coat,
But when she came back
  He was riding a goat.

She went to the cobbler's
  To buy him some shoes,
But when she came back
  He was reading the news.

She went to the seamstress
  To buy him some linen,
But when she came back
  The Dog was a-spinning.

She went to the hosier's
  To buy him some hose,
But when she came back
  He was dressed in his clothes.

The Dame made a curtsey,
  The Dog made a bow;
The Dame said, "Your servant,"
  The Dog said "Bow wow."

She went to the hatter's
  To buy him a hat,
But when she came back
  He was feeding the cat.

She went to the barber's
  To buy him a wig,
But when she came back
  He was dancing a jig.

Jingles

Higglety, pigglety, pop!
The dog has eaten the mop;
  The pig's in a hurry,
  The cat's in a flurry,
Higglety, pigglety, pop!

  —Peter Parley (Samuel Griswold Goodrich,) 1793–1860

Rub-a-dub-dub,
  Three men in a tub,
And how do you think they got there?
  The butcher, the baker,
  The candlestick-maker,
  They all jumped out of a rotten potato,
'Twas enough to make a man stare.

  —Mother Goose

POEMS

The Land of Counterpane

When I was sick and lay a-bed,
I had two pillows at my head,
And all my toys beside me lay
To keep me happy all the day.

And sometimes for an hour or so
I watched my leaden soldiers go,
With different uniforms and drills,
Among the bed-clothes, through the hills;

And sometimes sent my ships in fleets
All up and down among the sheets;
Or brought my trees and houses out,
And planted cities all about.

I was the giant great and still
That sits upon the pillow-hill,
And sees before him, dale and plain,
The pleasant land of counterpane.

—A Child's Garden of Verses
Robert Louis Stevenson, 1885

Rice Pudding

What is the matter with Mary Jane?
She's crying with all her might and main,
And she won't eat her dinner—rice pudding again—
What *is* the matter with Mary Jane?

What is the matter with Mary Jane?
I've promised her dolls and a daisy-chain,
And a book about animals—all in vain—
What *is* the matter with Mary Jane?

What is the matter with Mary Jane?
She's perfectly well, and she hasn't a pain;
But, look at her, now she's beginning again!—
What *is* the matter with Mary Jane?

What is the matter with Mary Jane?
I've promised her sweets and a ride in the train,
And I've begged her to stop for a bit and explain—
What *is* the matter with Mary Jane?

What is the matter with Mary Jane?
She's perfectly well and she hasn't a pain,
And it's lovely rice pudding for dinner again!—
What *is* the matter with Mary Jane?

—When We Were Very Young
A. A. Milne, 1924
(for Christopher Robin Milne)

The Duel

I have taught this poem hundreds of times: children invariably love it.

> —Poems Every Child Should Know
> *Mary E. Burt, 1904*

The gingham dog and the calico cat
Side by side on the table sat;
'Twas half-past twelve, and (what do you think!)
Nor one nor t'other had slept a wink!
The old Dutch clock and the Chinese plate
Appeared to know as sure as fate
There was going to be a terrible spat.
(I wasn't there; I simply state
What was told to me by the Chinese plate.)

The gingham dog went "bow-wow-wow!"
And the calico cat replied "mee-ow!"
The air was littered, an hour or so,
With bits of gingham and calico,
While the old Dutch clock in the chimney-place
Up with its hands before its face,
For it always dreaded a family row!
(Now mind: I'm only telling you
What the old Dutch clock declares is true!)

The Chinese plate looked very blue,
And wailed, "Oh, dear! what shall we do!"
But the gingham dog and the calico cat
Wallowed this way and tumbled that,
Employing every tooth and claw
In the awfullest way you ever saw—
And, oh! how the gingham and calico flew!
(Don't fancy I exaggerate!
I got my views from the Chinese plate!)

Next morning where the two had sat
They found no trace of the dog or cat;
And some folks think unto this day
That burglars stole the pair away!
But the truth about the cat and the pup
Is this: They ate each other up!
Now what do you really think of that!
(The old Dutch clock it told me so,
And that is how I came to know.)

> —Eugene Field, 1850–1895

The Owl and the Pussy-Cat

I.

The Owl and the Pussy-Cat went to sea
  In a beautiful pea-green boat,
They took some honey, and plenty of money,
  Wrapped up in a five-pound note.
The Owl looked up to the stars above,
  And sang to a small guitar,
"O lovely Pussy! O Pussy, my love,
  "What a beautiful Pussy you are,
    "You are,
    "You are!
  "What a beautiful Pussy you are!"

II.

Pussy said to the Owl, "You elegant fowl!
  "How charmingly sweet you sing!
"O let us be married! too long we have tarried:
  "But what shall we do for a ring?"
They sailed away for a year and a day,
  To the land where the Bong-tree grows,
And there in a wood a Piggy-wig stood,
  With a ring at the end of his nose,
    His nose,
    His nose,
  With a ring at the end of his nose.

III.

"Dear Pig, are you willing to sell for one shilling
  "Your ring?" Said the Piggy, "I will."
So they took it away, and were married next day
  By the Turkey who lives on the hill.
They dinèd on mince, and slices of quince,
  Which they ate with a runcible spoon;
And hand in hand, on the edge of the sand,
  They danced by the light of the moon,
    The moon,
    The moon,
  They danced by the light of the moon.

—Edward Lear, 1812–1888

PRAYERS

Mealtime

The Hampton Grace

God is great, God is good.
And we thank Him for this food.
By His hand must all be fed;
Give us, Lord, our daily bread.

While the earth remaineth,
Seedtime and harvest,
And cold and heat,
And summer and winter,
And day and night
Shall not cease.

—*Genesis 8:22*
(God's promise to Noah after the flood)

Bedtime

Now I lay me down to sleep
I pray thee, God, thy child to keep;
Thy love stay with me all the night,
And wake me with the morning light.

Now I lay me down to sleep
I pray the Lord my soul to keep;
All through the night may angels spread
Protecting wings above my bed.
Bless those I love, and those who love me
And grant us joy in serving Thee
God bless Mommy, Daddy . . .
And God bless me.

Jesus, tender Shepherd hear me;
Bless Thy little lamb tonight;
Through the darkness be Thou near me,
Watch my sleep till morning light.

Twenty-Third Psalm

The Lord is my shepherd; I shall not want.
He maketh me to lie down in green pastures:
He leadeth me beside the still waters.

He restoreth my soul, He leadeth me in the paths
of righteousness for His name's sake.

Yea, though I walk through the valley of the shadow
of death, I will fear no evil: for Thou art with me;
Thy rod and Thy staff they comfort me.

Thou preparest a table before me in the presence of
mine enemies: Thou anointest my head with oil;
my cup runneth over.

Surely goodness and mercy shall follow me all the
days of my life, and I will dwell in the house of
the Lord for ever.

The Pilot Psalm

The Lord is my Pilot. I shall not drift.

He lighteth me across the dark waters; He steereth
me in the deep channels; He keepeth my log.

He guideth me by the Star of Holiness for
His name's sake.

Yea, though I sail 'mid the thunders and tempests
of life I will dread no danger, for Thou art with
me; Thy love and Thy care, they shelter me.

Thou preparest a harbour before me in the homeland
of eternity; Thou anointest the waves with oil;
my ship rideth calmly.

Surely sunlight and starlight shall favour me on the
voyage I take, and I will anchor in the port of my
God for ever.

—*Anonymous*

STORIES

The innermost desire of a vigorous, genuine child is to understand his life. This he cannot do by comparing himself with himself. For clarity, he needs a mirror to the outside world.

This is why children so need and love stories, legends and tales. Stories concern other men, other times and places, but the listening child is suddenly free to look for his own image, safe in the knowledge that no one else knows what it is that he seeks.

We do not tell our children enough stories. At best, we tell little stories with mechanical heroes, puppets which we ourselves have stuffed or whittled.

—The Education of Man
Friedrich Froebel, 1826

The insights of Froebel into the unfolding of a child's selfhood enabled him to organize the method of infant education to which he, in 1840, gave the name of "Kindergarten" from the German, "the garden of children."

—W. T. Harris, *in Translator's Preface to the 1887 American edition of* The Education of Man

A mother barely realizes how soon she begins storytelling. When she sings "Hush Little Baby" to her two-month-old, she is telling him a story. The same happens when she claps "Pat-a-Cake" with her six-month-old. A two-year-old sees a story in a single picture. A story as such is only a more formal word structure than the child has until then been used to.

We read to our children, but many of the stories are bland and colorless. Too often, they are as safe as a Mickey Mouse cartoon. Some recent stories are exceptional and will last; but to sort out the good from the useless, a mother should read a story by herself before buying it or borrowing it from the library.

Many children's classics are still in print, but too often they have been rewritten and emasculated beyond recognition. A mother should choose old stories carefully too, making sure the writing and illustrations are still vivid and alive.

The old stories were often very matter-of-fact about violence and tragedy. Parents and authors now seem desperate to protect small children from any knowledge of greed, cruelty, death and the like. But children sense all of life's dangers sooner than we want to admit. As long as they end happily, suspenseful fairy tales can help a child be less afraid. They give him a way to play out in his mind the horrors he dares not talk about.

Not all old stories deserve to survive. "Babes in the Woods" was an unneces-

sarily terrifying tale of two small innocents left to starve (which they did) in the forest. But Mother Goose's "Death and Burial of Poor Cock Robin" ("Who'll be the parson? . . . Who'll toll the bell?" etc.) was read to generations of children who would then act out the story. Granted, families were larger, and a big brother could assign roles and safely lead the way. But even the littlest helped ritualize death in singsong and reduce it to manageable child-world proportions.

I think some of Aesop, the Brothers Grimm, Hans Christian Anderson, Beatrix Potter and other classic authors should still be the backbone of a child's story world. In this short space, I have concentrated on old stories, and especially on authors who are not currently popular but who deserve to be revived.

I have also included a Greek myth, a Bible tale and a history story because a child should be exposed to a wider range of literature than just fairy tales. Even a very small child can become absorbed in a well-told Egyptian legend, an oriental parable, Indian fables, Viking myths or tales of medieval chivalry. It is admittedly hard to find simple, evocative store-bought versions. Years ago, parents and grandparents told such stories from memory—and we can still do that. If a mother or father remembers the story of Charlemagne or Davey Crockett, he or she can tell it aloud. If the parent tells it simply, the child will ask for it again and again, wanting more explicit details as he grows.

Reading or storytelling time is special. It creates a quiet sense of family intimacy that lasts long past the early years. We depend mostly on books now, but sitting side by side with a child over a book is time never wasted. It results in one of the greatest gifts an adult can give a child: the love of reading.

A Lion and a Mouse

A mouse one day happened to run across the paws of a sleeping Lion and wakened him. The Lion, angry at being disturbed, grabbed the Mouse and was about to swallow him when the Mouse cried out, "Please, kind Sir, I didn't mean it; if you will let me go, I shall always be grateful, and perhaps I can help you someday."

The idea that such a little thing as a Mouse could help him so amused the Lion that he let the Mouse go.

A week later the Mouse heard a Lion roaring loudly. He went closer to see what the trouble was and found his Lion caught in a hunter's net. Remembering his promise, the Mouse began to gnaw the ropes of the net and kept it up until the Lion could get free. The Lion then acknowledged that little friends might prove great friends.

—*Aesop, c. 620–c. 560* B.C.

The Elves and the Shoemaker

There was once an honest, hard-working shoemaker who could not seem to earn enough money to support himself and his wife. At last, he had only enough leather to make one more pair of shoes. Very discouraged, he cut out the leather pieces one night and went to bed. He planned to sew them together in the morning.

When the man sat down at his shoemaker's bench the next morning, he saw a beautiful pair of shoes, already sewn together. Amazed, he looked at the work carefully, but there was not a stitch out of place.

Soon a customer came in, saw the shoes, and paid a high price for them. The shoemaker then took the money and bought enough leather to make two more pairs. That night, he again cut out the leather pieces and went to bed.

In the morning, he found two handsome pairs of shoes on the table, ready to sell. Buyers came in and paid him well for both. So, late in the day, the shoemaker went out and bought leather for four more pairs of shoes. That night, he again cut out the pieces and went to sleep. The next day, the shoes were finished as before.

The magic went on for many days—whatever work the shoemaker got ready at night was always finished at dawn. The shoes sold well, and before long the man was rich.

When the Christmas season came that year, the shoemaker and his wife wanted very much to find out who was doing all this good work. One night, instead of going to bed as usual, they left a candle burning in the workroom and hid themselves behind a curtain close by.

At exactly midnight, in came two little elves. They sat upon the shoemaker's bench, and soon their little fingers were quickly stitching and rapping and tapping. When the job was done, the elves put the finished shoes on the table and ran away into the night.

The astonished shoemaker and his wife came out from behind the curtain. "Those elves have made us rich," said the wife. "I would like to do something for them in return."

"I know!" she exclaimed. "The little men seem to have very few clothes for this cold weather. I'll make them each a shirt, a vest, a jacket and a pair of pantaloons. And you can make them each a little pair of shoes."

The shoemaker liked the idea. He and his wife went to bed feeling happy.

In a few days they had the clothes ready. That evening they left no work on the bench, but laid out the small outfits instead. Then they hid behind the curtain again to watch.

At midnight, the elves came in and went to the bench as usual. Suddenly they saw the tiny clothes. They began to laugh and make merry noises. They dressed themselves from top to toe, and then danced and capered and sprang around the room. Without warning, they skipped out the door and disappeared down the lane.

The shoemaker and his wife never saw the elves again, but everything went well for them as long as they lived.

—The Brothers Grimm

Fanny Overkind

Fanny Overkind thought she could never be kind enough, but the fact was she tried much too hard.

One day, a poor and hungry boy came to her house with a basket, asking for a bit of cold leftover meat. Kind Fanny went to the kitchen and brought him a large piece of plum cake instead, which he ate up immediately. But he was not used to such rich food, and he made himself very sick.

Fanny Watering her Little Garden.

Fanny Giving a Poor Boy Plum Cake.

Fanny had a little garden that she took good care of, or at least she thought she did. When little birds began picking at the plants, Fanny found a net to cover her flowers and keep the birds away. But the birds were only picking off the caterpillars and bugs that were going to eat the young plants. If Fanny had not put the net over her garden, the plants would not have died.

Fanny Frighted at the Mice.

Mice and rats decided to live in Fanny's house, but she thought it was cruel to trap them or scare them off. So when she sat down to dinner, she had all the mice and rats in the house to help her eat it.

Little Fanny Leading the Horse Along.

One day, Fanny saw an old horse pulling a vegetable cart along the road. An old woman was taking the horse and cart to market, but Fanny decided to help them along. She tried to pull the horse by the reins, but the horse reached for Fanny's new straw hat and ate it right off her head.

—*Anonymous, adapted from:* Pictures and Stories from Forgotten Children's Books, *by Arnold Arnold, 1969*

When it rained, Fanny would go out with a large umbrella and try to keep it over a brood of young ducks so that they would not get wet. What she didn't understand was that ducks like to be in water sometimes. And they certainly like rain.

Little Fanny and her Young Ducks.

Fanny had a canary bird, but she thought it was unfair to keep him in a cage. He was too young to fly very far, so when she let him out he flew a little ways and then lighted on the ground. Fanny also had a cat. When the cat saw the bird, he caught him and killed him. Poor Fanny had a funeral for the canary bird and buried him in the garden, under a rose bush.

Fanny Leting the Bird out of its Cage.

The Funeral of Fanny's Dickey Bird.

The Nutcracker Dwarf

One day two boys were out gathering hazelnuts in the woods. They sat down under a tree to eat them, but they did not have their knives, and they could not crack the nuts with their teeth.

"Oh," they complained, "if only someone would come and open the nuts for us."

Hardly had they said this when a little man came through the woods—and such a strange little man! He had a great, great head, and from the back of it a thin pigtail hung down to his heels. He wore a golden cap, a red coat and yellow stockings. As he came near he sang:

"Hight! Hight! Bite! Bite!
Hans hight I! Nuts bite I!
I chase squirrels through the trees,
I gather nuts just as I please,
I place them 'twixt my jaws so strong,
And crack and eat them all day long!"

Even though the boys knew the little man was probably a troublesome Wood Dwarf, they laughed at the way he looked.

They called out to him, "If you know how to crack nuts, come and open ours."

But the little man grumbled through his long white beard:

"If I crack the nuts for you,
Promise that you'll give me two."

"Yes, yes," cried the boys, "you shall have all the nuts you wish. Only do crack them for us."

Because of his stiff pigtail, he could not sit down, so he stood before the boys and sang:

"Lift my pigtail, long and thin,
Place your nuts my jaws within,
Pull the pigtail down, and then
I'll crack your nuts, my little men."

The boys did as they were told, laughing all the while at the dwarf's funny game. They put nut after nut in his mouth, pulled down on the pigtail, and each time a broken nut popped out of the Nutcracker's mouth.

Soon all the hazelnuts were opened. The boys were chewing them happily when the little man began to grumble:

"Hight! Hight! Bite! Bite!
Your nuts are cracked, and now my pay
I'll take, and then I'll go away."

Now one of the boys wished to give the little man his promised reward, but the other boy, a greedy fellow, stopped him, saying, "Why give that old man our nuts? There really are only enough for us. Nutcracker, go away and find some nuts for yourself."

Then the little man grew angry and grumbled horribly:

"If you do not pay me fee,
Why, then, you've told a lie to me!
I am hungry, you're well fed,
Quick, or I'll bite off your head!"

But the boy who did not want to give the nuts away only laughed and said, "You'll bite off my head, will you? Go away from here just as fast as you can or you will feel these nutshells!" He scooped some up and shook a fistful at the little man.

The Nutcracker grew red with rage. He pulled down his pigtail, snapped his jaws together—crack—and off came the greedy boy's head.

—Count Franz Pocci, 1807–1876

King Midas and the Golden Touch

Hundreds of years ago in a country called Greece, there lived a king named Midas. His palace was surrounded by beautiful rose gardens, for he was king of a part of Greece called Phrygia, the land of roses.

As he walked in his gardens one morning, he discovered a sad, rumpled-looking stranger sleeping among the flowers. King Midas brought the man back to the palace, saw that he was fed and well taken care of.

When the stranger felt better, he revealed that he was one of the followers of the great god Dionysos. Now the Greeks worshiped many gods, but Dionysos was one of the most powerful. Midas soon took the man back to where the god lived. Dionysos was so grateful for this kindness that he told the king he would grant him any wish.

King Midas thought a moment. Even though he was rich indeed, the one thing he wanted was more gold.

"Oh," answered Midas, "if only I could turn everything I touched into gold!"

"From tomorrow on," said the god, "everything you touch shall become gold."

That night the king could hardly sleep for joy. In the morning, he raised his purple robe to put it around his shoulders. Instantly, every thread was golden. He sat down to fasten his sandals. First the chair he was sitting in became golden. Then when he bent down to fasten his sandals, they too changed, from leather to gold.

When King Midas strolled in his garden that morning, every rose he passed became a golden flower. Even the path he walked on became a carpet of gold.

Happy as he was, the king finally became hungry, so he went back to the palace for breakfast. Thirstily, he picked up his water goblet. But as he put it to his lips, the goblet and the water both turned to gold. He tried to eat, but every forkful of food changed into a chunk of solid gold.

Suddenly King Midas realized that the gift of the golden touch was horrible. If he could not get rid of it, he would starve and die.

He hurried back to Dionysos.

"Are you not happy, King Midas?" asked the god.

"I am most miserable," groaned the king. "I cannot eat. I cannot drink. I beg you to take away this hateful touch."

Dionysos felt sorry for the king. He told him to go and bathe in a certain river, and that after his bath the touch would be gone.

Midas ran to the river. As he stood in the water, he could feel the golden touch washing off him. Afterward, back to his palace he went, a contented man.

If you go to the banks of that river in Greece, it is said that you will still find tiny grains of gold in the sand.

—from the Greek myths
set down by Ovid and others

The Prodigal Son
The Wasteful Son

Long ago in Palestine, a hot country on the Mediterranean Sea, there lived a man named Jesus. He called Himself the Son of God. So gentle and wise was He that enormous crowds followed Him, asking Him to teach them about God.

The important people in that land were called the Pharisees, and they were trying to decide whether they should allow Jesus to call himself the Son of God. They listened to His teachings, but they didn't like having to sit next to the poor people, the sick people, the beggars and even the thieves who surrounded Him. But Jesus welcomed everyone, even criminals, when they wanted to be forgiven for the things they felt they had done wrong. To help the proud Pharisees understand, Jesus told them this story or parable:

There was once a wealthy farmer who had two sons. The younger son grew unhappy in his father's house and wanted to leave. But before he left, he asked his father to give him all the money that he would have inherited after his father died. The father did not question his son but simply gave him the money.

The young man went to a distant country. There he lived wildly, spent his father's money quickly, and refused to think about the years ahead. But soon a famine fell upon the land; there was not enough rain, and the crops in the field withered and died.

Before he knew it, the young man was a beggar. He was so poor that he felt very lucky when a farmer in that far country agreed to let him go into the fields and take care of the pigs. But the young man earned little money and was always so hungry that he nearly began to eat the little bit of corn that the pigs left among the husks.

One day the young man realized how lonely he was and how foolishly he had wasted his father's money.

"I will go back to my father," he said. "I will tell him I am sorry. I don't think he will ever forgive me, but I will ask him just to let me be one of his servants."

So he traveled home, and his father saw him coming. The father was so glad to see his son that he ran to meet him, kissed him, and forgave him.

And the son said unto him,
"Father, I have sinned against
heaven, and in thy sight, and
am no more worthy to be called
thy son."

—*Luke 15:21*

But his father gave him new clothes and arranged for a great feast that night to welcome him home.

That evening, the older son came back from the fields where he had been working all day. He heard music and singing coming from his father's house and didn't understand what was happening. A servant told him that his brother had come home and that his father was celebrating.

When he heard this, the older son became jealous and angry and would not go inside. It did not seem fair to him that his foolish brother should be welcomed home so happily. His father came outside to talk to him.

"All the time that my brother has been gone," said the older son, "I have worked for you faithfully. But never have you arranged a feast for me."

The father loved both his sons and tried to explain:

"Son, thou are ever with me, and all
I have is thine.
It is meet that we should
make merry, and be glad: for
this thy brother was dead, and
is alive again; and was lost, and
is found."

—*Luke 15:31,32*

In the Bible, that is where the story ends. Jesus went no further because he felt sure the Pharisees would understand that the father was like God. The father loved his son because his son was admitting his mistakes. God loved the beggars and thieves who followed Jesus because they wanted to change their miserable lives. Only the older son, like the Pharisees, needed to learn to forgive his brother.

—*adapted from the Gospel of Luke, chapter 15*

Christopher Columbus and His Frightened Sailors

A long time ago, the people in Europe wanted the jewels, sweet spices and silk that came from faraway India, China and Japan. To get these riches, traders went east over land, through deserts, and across small seas. But the journey was long, and the people grew impatient.

A bright, young sailor named Christopher Columbus was living at that time. He thought that if he sailed a boat west, across the wide Atlantic Ocean, he could get to India faster than anyone else.

People laughed at Christopher Columbus. In Italy, the country where he lived, many people thought no one could sail the Atlantic Ocean and come home alive. They still believed the earth was not round but flat, and that Columbus would fall off the edge.

Columbus needed money to buy ships and supplies for his journey, but the rich people didn't want to waste their money. To get rid of Columbus, they called him a fool.

"If you could sail to the bottom of the world," they joked, "you'd only find people who walk upside down."

"Besides," they warned, "to get to the other side of the world you have to sail through fiery waters. The waves will be boiling hot."

But Columbus knew this was not true. So he went to a nearby country named Spain to ask King Ferdinand and Queen Isabella for the money he needed. But here too he had to wait and wait and wait for an answer. Finally the king and queen decided to give Columbus the money to make his trip.

In Fourteen hundred and ninety-two,
Columbus sailed the ocean blue.

The Niña, the Pinta and the Santa Maria, three sturdy sailing ships with good, brave crews on board, left the coast of Spain one day in autumn. It was not a hard journey. They sailed by a southern route, and the weather was fine. The winds kept the sails billowing.

However, as the days passed, the sailors began to worry. They saw a whale and thought it was a sea monster. They saw an island volcano spewing fire and were sure there were boiling waters just ahead. They wanted to turn back.

To calm the sailors, Captain Columbus crossed over from one boat to another to show the maps he had made. He knew the bread and water supplies were growing low. He knew the sailors might get so angry they would tie him to the mast and turn the boats around themselves.

"Give me three more days," said Columbus. "If we do not sight land by then, we will go back."

The sailors agreed.

Just before the three days were up, a lookout high up in the rigging cried out, "Land, ho!" The sailors heard the news and wept with happiness.

The ships set anchor near a green and tropical shore. Columbus dressed himself in a red military uniform embroidered with gold. Then he rowed ashore in a small boat with the captains of the other two boats and a small military guard.

When they reached the sandy beach, Columbus threw himself on his knees and kissed the ground. He held up the cross of Christianity and King Ferdinand's royal standard and claimed the land in the name of Spain.

Columbus thought he was in India. When he saw the naked native people who lived there, he called them Indians.

Columbus did not find India. He found a warm island named San Salvador that belonged to the big new continent which we call the Americas. He did not find the mountains of precious stones or pearl-covered beaches he had hoped for, but he found the New World.

Columbus sailed safely back to Spain and told everyone of his adventures. From that time on, people did believe the world was round. And they began to dream about the beautiful land that was waiting for them across the wide Atlantic Ocean.

—adapted from A Brief History of the United States,
Barnes' Historical Series, 1871

PLAYTIME

We cannot depend on beautiful toys to keep a child's curiosity alive. Perfect toys are not really interesting unless destroyed in order to learn their secrets. If the child is left alone, this work will often be undertaken.

—Studies in Invalid Occupation
Susan E. Tracy, 1910

The poor quality and endless quantity of American toys have become a household nightmare. Some toys are still "beautiful," but a mother cannot lean on them to cultivate a child's play world. To fight the toy mountain monster, a mother should buy fewer and more durable toys. She should also stockpile some simple ideas for toys to make, play projects and easy games.

Cheap toys usually break within hours of purchase. Others have seventeen tiny parts which a young child will inevitably scatter around his room. The child's room or even the whole house becomes impossible to neaten, and the clean-up conflict between mother and child worsens daily.

If a child had only a set of blocks, a blackboard and chalk, stuffed animals and dolls, he would use them with endless variety. He would also be relieved of the guilt of broken and lost toys and would be more willing to help pick up at the end of the day.

Furniture made from paper boxes. Dishes of leather and tin foil.

Unfortunately, it is almost impossible now to keep a child's toy life simple. Our children are bombarded with toy advertisements. They see that all the other kids have mounds of toys, so why can't they? Mothers are also partly to blame. They feel they don't know enough things to do with children, so they buy toys instead. I once knew a mother who was delighted with her system of buying "just something little" for her child every single day. To me, the child looked like a hyperactive mess. I couldn't help but think that the mother was using cheap toys to keep the child at arm's length rather than letting him enter her life.

Many of us are frightened of our children because we think they will ask too much of us, and we don't know how to give. Having a small arsenal of rainy afternoon ideas reassures a mother. Their purpose should be to get a child started on something that will absorb his attention without the mother constantly having to participate.

Some very old childhood staples are still much in use. Mothers still help children with crayons, finger paints, beads and such, but other easy, inexpensive homemade toys and pastimes are being forgotten. Paper hats, bean bag games and water experiments are not complicated.

I have concentrated on projects that need only things around the house for the making: wood, paper, scissors and the like. Many of them can be thrown away after the child's interest wanes. Paper doll chains and button card people need not clutter a child's room for months; they can always be made again. Also, the simple construction of such games as a nail board and rubber bands or the marble bridge board saves a mother hours of fruitless toy repair and hunting for missing parts.

To keep a child's room manageable, a mother has to be a gentle despot. If someone gives your child a real watch when he is only two years old, store it in a drawer. If he is given a race track set with thirty lengths of badly fitting plastic track and needing four batteries, simply remove it altogether. Also, a child's toys can be rotated. When the child asks for a toy he one day realizes is not in his room, bring it out, and quietly store away something he is tired of. Most important, establish a time of day when mother and child clean things up, together.

We all have to fight the easy-buying impulse and the television-baby-sitter syndrome. But we can't fight unless we have weapons. The weapons here can be used gently, but they will help push away the unseen, mechanized, computerized-play robot. The robot is killing our children's innate, private world of play.

"How Many Fingers" Game

The child lays his head in his mother's lap (which is easier for a small child than trying to close his eyes). With one hand, the mother holds up one or more fingers. With the other, she claps the child on the back and chants:

Mingledy, mingledy, clap, clap,
How many fingers do I hold up?

The child guesses. If he is wrong, the mother says:

Three you said, and two it was,
Mingledy, mingledy, clap, clap,
How many fingers do I hold up?

When the child guesses correctly, it is his turn to make his mother close her eyes and try to guess.

This is a very simple play, and can be understood by children of three years old. . . . But the thumbs must never be held up.

—American Girl's Book
by Miss Leslie, 1838

Dice

MATERIALS
two dice

Of the dozens of dice games that can be played, at least one works with a small child. Mother and child each take one die. The mother explains that whoever throws and gets a "one" wins a point. She keeps score, either aloud or on paper. "One" works well in the beginning, but other numbers may be used.

If the child is ready for more complications, name a number which takes a point away from the score. In fact, you can change the game every time the child plays. His endurance and concentration are what mat-ter. Because a dice game can be changed or stopped when the child gets itchy, it is no problem to him. If the child is having trouble learning how to "lose" in board games (e.g., failing to reach "Home," as in Parcheesi), a dice game will be less frustrating. Also, he can play it with an older brother or sister.

Older children may throw two dice at a time and write down the sum of combinations: for example, $4 + 3 = 7$. The same device may be used later in subtraction or multiplication.

—Education by Play and Games
George Ellsworth Johnson, 1907

Nail Board and Rubber Band Game

MATERIALS
*a piece of wood, manageable size, at least 2" thick—
    may be square, rectangular or odd-shaped*
nails, 2" or longer
hammer
rubber bands of different thicknesses and colors

MAKING THE BOARD
Furnish the materials and mark the places on the board for the nails. The two-year-old will want to do some of the hammering. The four-year-old will want to help design the nail pattern and do much more pounding. In the end, be sure the nails protrude about an inch, are secure and are spaced at least one inch away from each other.

THE GAME
The child stretches the rubber bands up, down and across the board. If he loads five on the same set of nails, the mother can suggest how to vary the design. The board may become a ferry boat, a musical instrument or a play machine.

When the child tires of the game for the day, remove the rubber bands for him. He won't. Bring out the rubber bands only for game time, or the child will be tempted to throw them around the room.

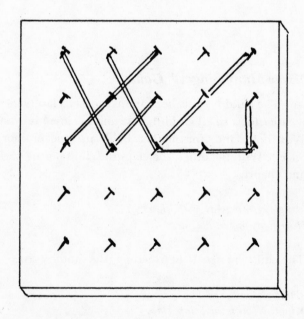

NAIL BOARD AND RUBBER BAND GAME

Smell Boxes

MATERIALS
small boxes with lids
scotch tape
scissors and/or safety pin
anything small and aromatic, e.g.:
> *cinnamon sticks*
> *coffee beans*
> *whole black peppercorns*
> *celery seed*
> *tea*
> *whole cloves*
> *lemon peel*
> *cedar shavings*
> *lilac flowers*
> *rose petals*
> *apple blossoms*
> *geranium leaves*
> *carnation*
> *onion grass*
> *gardenia*
> *violets*

TO MAKE THE BOXES

Put something strong-smelling in the box and tape it shut. Poke holes in the top, large holes for large contents, such as cinnamon sticks, small holes for things like celery seed.

THE GAME

Give the child the box and ask him to guess what's inside. Write the name of the ingredient on the bottom. Making even one box is fun, especially one filled with peppercorns, because it can be called "the stinky box" or some such. But the more boxes the merrier. Your own kitchen spices are easiest, but use whatever scent sources are handy in your house.

This play can include other games for sense training: identification of substances by taste, by touch, or of objects struck or dropped.

—Education by Play and Games
George Ellsworth Johnson, 1907

Scrapbook

MATERIALS
loose-leaf binder with paper
pictures
scissors
glue or scotch tape

THE SCRAPBOOK

Even a two-year-old likes to work, briefly, on his own scrapbook. The older preschooler may become so absorbed he will want titles written under the pictures, or his own "stories" put down under each page.

Collect funny, lively or just beautiful color illustrations from magazines. Save postcards, any extra photographs of family doings, birthday cards and so on. These help the child remember his own happiest growing times.

At scrapbook time, bring out the pictures and let the child choose the ones he wants. Help the two-year-old cut the magazine pictures. Let an older child do as much cutting as he can. Only after the picture choosing and cutting is done, bring out the glue or tape.

The advantage of a loose-leaf binder is that the pages can be taken out, drowned in glue, painted on or crayoned. Once they are dry, the pages can be put back. Small children are hard on paper: you will need reinforcements for the ring holes. Then you can turn the pages as often as the child wants to reread his scrapbook.

Understand that the main object is to amuse, not to produce results. If you expect the young child to make a nice picture book, either you will be woefully disappointed, or be obliged to do the main part of it yourself.

—Twenty-Six Hours a Day
Mary Blake, 1883

Soft Playdough

MATERIALS

2 cups flour
⅔ cup salt
2 tbs. oil
1 cup water
food color

TO MAKE

Mix flour, salt and oil. A little at a time, add pre-colored water (10 or 12 drops of food color at least) and mix again until the dough feels workable. If the dough gets soggy, add more flour. If it seems too dry, add a bit more water. Even half the amounts in the recipe make enough for one child to use. What makes this playdough non-drying is the oil. Keep it in a covered container in the refrigerator, and it will last several weeks or more.

THE GAME

Let the child help make the dough. That's playtime in itself. Then let him squeeze, pound, poke and wrestle with the dough. Provide cookie cutters, a rolling pin, a garlic press to make "spaghetti," toothpicks for birthday candles or whatever else seems to spur the child on.

Playdough is being sold commercially, but this kind is easier and softer for a small child. It's also less expensive, more exciting for the child since he can help make it, and simpler for the mother because there's only one color mixture to deal with at a time.

Hard Playdough

MATERIALS

2 cups flour
1 cup salt
1 cup water (approx.)

TO MAKE

Mix the flour and salt. Add the water, a little at a time. If the mixture seems too mushy, add flour. If it gets too crumbly, add water.

TO PLAY

This dough is less sticky than the non-drying kind and very satisfying to the sense of touch. However, it should be used soon after the making. Again, let the child make his own squishy shapes. Because the dough can be painted and shellacked when dry, encourage the child to use it to make presents for his father's birthday (e.g., his hand imprint), for Christmas ornaments, etc.

The dough can either be left to dry by itself for a few days, or it can be cooked in a medium oven for 45 minutes or so, until slightly brown. Paint when cool. Shellac when dry.

Put a potato before the child. Have him make an egg-shaped likeness. Encourage him to add 'eyes.' Why? Because the farmer plants the eye parts, from each of which another potato plant will grow.

—Kindergarten at Home
V. M. Hillyer, 1911

Early Advice

The play tendencies which we stigmatize as "evil" in little children are often merely those which cause annoyance to us adults. Not understanding their needs, we try to prevent their every movement, their every attempt to gain experience for themselves, especially by touching everything.

If we block the child's natural need to co-ordinate his movements and collect impressions and sensations, he will inevitably rebel. If we provoke him far enough, he will show violent manifestations of his very real struggle for existence.

—Dr. Montessori's Own Handbook
Maria Montessori, 1914

Ringtoss

MATERIALS
piece of wood, 12" or so square, 1" thick
dowel approx. 8" long
screwdriver and 2" screw
heavy rope
masking tape, string, or needle and heavy thread

TO MAKE

From the bottom, screw the board and dowel together. The rings should be at least 8 inches in diameter (larger than most being sold in sets now, and easier for children). Cut lengths of rope and sew, tape or wind the ends together with string. Winding the rings with strips of colored cloth or ribbon makes them more interesting. Rings of different sizes are also good.

THE GAME

The child should stand as close to the upright post as necessary in order to be successful at least some of the time. If he's playing inside, mark the throwing spot with tape on the floor. Outside, use chalk or draw a line in the dirt. Make up your own simple rules about scoring and numbers of turns according to how many children are playing, their ages and their persistence.

Bean Bag Games

TO MAKE BEAN BAGS

Anyone can sew bean bags instead of buying them. Make it a comfortable size for the child's hand, in any shape from a square to a frog design. After sewing two pieces of material together inside out, leaving enough open space to insert the contents, turn the bag right side out. Fill only about two-thirds of the way with any kind of dried beans, rice or corn. Sew up the opening. Even with hand sewing, these take only about fifteen minutes to make. Make three or four for a child so he can play any of the following bean bag games.

GAMES

1. Mark a standing spot on the floor and have the child or children throw bean bags into a wastebasket. Help them keep score.

2. Mark three concentric rings (like an archery target) on the floor (or ground). Have the child try to land the bag in the center.

3. Fasten three square or rectangular supermarket boxes together, the smallest inside, the largest outside. Poke holes through the bottoms of all three boxes and secure them with string.) Throwing into the biggest box counts one, into the middle box two, into the smallest box three.

The bags ought to weigh not less than half a pound.
—Education by Play and Games
George Ellsworth Johnson, 1907

Puzzles

MATERIALS
a large picture (magazine or other)
glue
cardboard
scissors

TO MAKE
Choose a picture you think the child would really be interested in. Glue it onto a heavy piece of cardboard. Cut the picture into large, odd-shaped pieces.

Carbon Paper

MATERIALS
a sheet of carbon paper
a supply of plain paper
pencil
clipboard or paper clips

TO PLAY
Show the child how to put the carbon paper, dark side down, between two sheets of plain paper. Secure all with the clipboard or paper clips. Give the child a pencil and tell him to draw a picture or scribble at will. It is magic when he finds a duplicate under the carbon paper.

When you're at the bank, let the child make out his own deposit slip (banks seem patient about this). Again the child will discover a carbon reproduction. If you're really lucky, the teller will even stamp the deposit slip for the child.

Paper Chains

MATERIALS
paper
scissors
glue

TO MAKE
If the child is young, cut colored paper strips (about 1″ x 6″) for him. Paste one strip end to end, then show him how to put in a second strip, bend it around, and glue the ends. A paste jar with a brush works well with a two- or three-year-old. He will need newspapers to work on.

The four- or five-year-old may want to make the strips himself. Give him a square piece of paper. Have him fold it in half three times (for a 6″ square), keeping the edges even and creasing them well with his fingernails. Then he can tear along the creased lines and end up with his own eight links. At this age, he can use a more liquid glue from a squeeze tube or plastic bottle.

Paper chains can be made for holidays (e.g., red and green for Christmas, orange and black for Halloween), but the child doesn't have to have a reason. He can use paper chains simply to decorate his room or a bulletin board. The older the child, the shorter and narrower the strips can be.

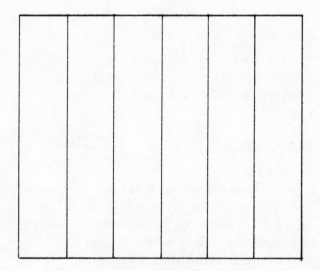

Paper Chains

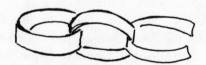

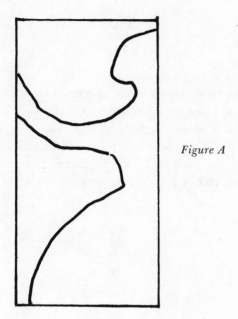

Figure A

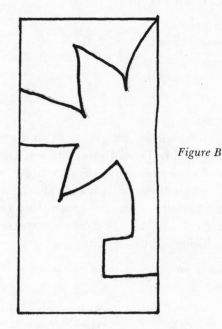

Figure B

Figure C

Paper Dolls

MATERIALS

*newspaper, left-over wrapping paper, or plain or
    colored sheets*

scissors

TO MAKE

Long narrow paper, not too heavy, works the best.
Fold the paper in half, then in half again, and again.
The more folds, the more paper dolls. Draw half a
figure—girl (Figure A), boy, soldier, animal or flower

(Figure B)—making sure that some part of each folded
edge is left uncut so there will be a connecting link.
Cut the figure out and unfold.

A mother can do this very quickly for a child, or
she can show him how to do it. His amount of doing
depends on what he thinks he's capable of accom-
plishing.

If you have chosen dancing figures, tape the two
ends together so they may dance in a circle.

Button Card People

MATERIALS
heavy paper or index cards
buttons of various sizes
needle and heavy thread
pen or crayon

TO MAKE
The simplest button card person has buttons for eyes, and a face and body drawn around them. Or there can be a medium button for the head, a larger one for the trunk, and smaller ones tapering off for arms and legs. Attach the buttons to the paper with needle and thread. (A child who has not been interested in sewing may suddenly want to try buttons.)

Place cards for a special dinner can be made with button-face people.

—Studies in Invalid Occupation
Susan E. Tracy, 1910

N.B.: An even simpler way to interest a child in sewing is to buy a sewing hoop. Insert a plain, light piece of material. Cut out a cloth banana, for example, and show the child how to attach it to the material. It only takes a few stitches. In the beginning, the child will ask with each stitch, "On top now, or under?"

A Cocked Hat

MATERIALS
a sheet of newspaper
straight pins or tape

TO MAKE
A. Fold the upper edge of the newspaper to the lower. B. Fold the right edge to left to make a vertical crease down the center. Open. C. Fold the upper right and left corners down so that they meet at the center line. D. First fold half the remaining bottom width of paper up, then fold the rest of each bottom side once more.

The hat can be worn as is, but to make it more secure, pin or tape the centerfold side together.
A tassel or plume pinned to the top of course makes the hat more gay.

—Kindergarten at Home
V. M. Hillyer, 1911

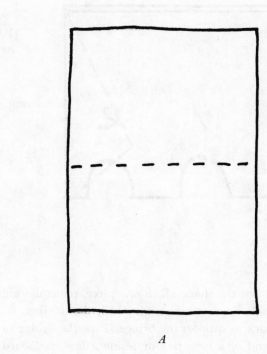

A

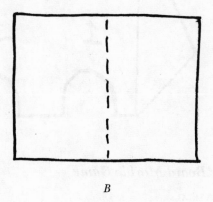

B

Cocked Hat

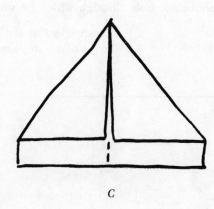

C

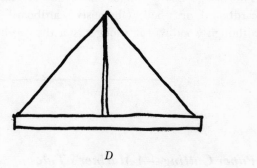

D

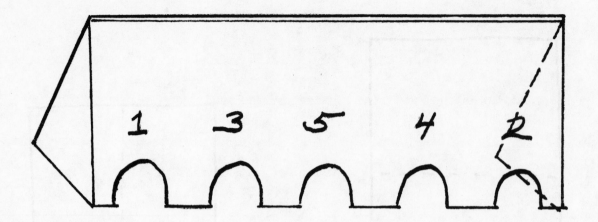

Bridge Board Marble Game

MATERIALS

a length of wood, can be 20" long, 4" high
2 wood triangle pieces 4"
hammer
nails
or cardboard 28" long (4" for each back support)
scissors
pen or pencil
tape
tray or cardboard box

TO MAKE

The bridge board can be made out of either heavy cardboard or wood. Obviously, cardboard is easier, although wood will last longer. For the cardboard ver-sion, cut out the shape all in one piece, remembering the triangle flaps at each end, which should then be folded back to support the bridge. Tape the bridge to the far end of a long tray or inside a low cardboard box with one end cut off. This way, the marbles won't roll all over the room.

TO PLAY

The game is to roll marbles through the arches from a given distance, the player scoring the number marked above the hole through which he shoots.

—Education by Play and Games
George Ellsworth Johnson, 1907

Paper Cutting—A Mariner's Tale

MATERIALS

square piece of paper (8" or so)
scissors

TO MAKE AND PLAY

Fold the paper in half, twice. Start from the center fold corner. As you cut Figure A, say to the child, "What does a captain need to help guide his boat at night?" A star unfolds.

As you cut Figure B, say to the child, "When the boat reaches shore, what do the sailors throw overboard?" An anchor (but do not unfold yet).

Finally, say to the child, "When the boat leaves the harbor, what does the captain need to steer with?" Let the anchor figure fall open and a steering wheel will emerge.

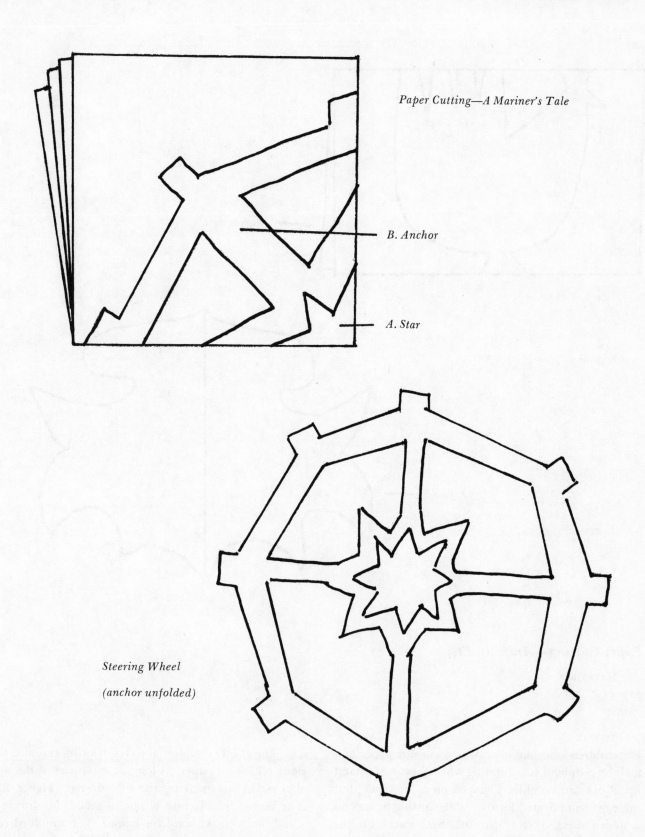

Paper Cutting—A Mariner's Tale

B. Anchor

A. Star

Steering Wheel

(anchor unfolded)

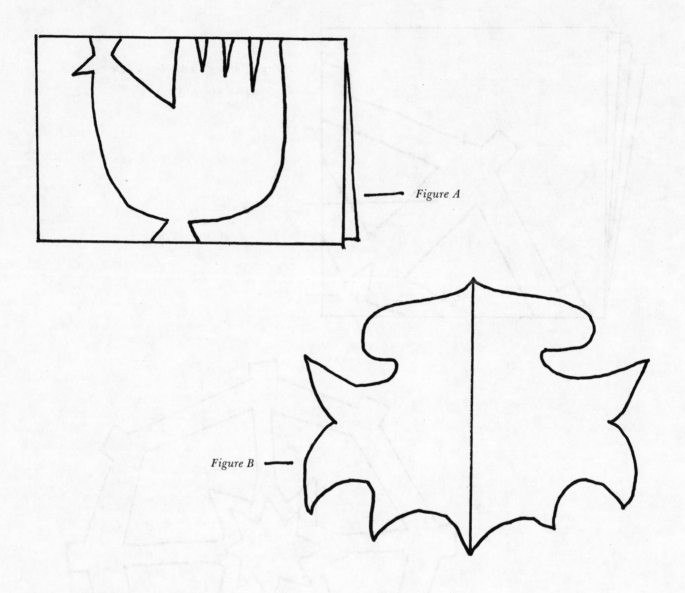

Figure A

Figure B

Paper Cutting—Animals, Etc.

MATERIALS

paper
scissors

TO MAKE

For children who like to draw and cut out paper animals or people, it is frustrating when they won't stand up. Props can be glued or taped on at the back, but these get complicated for the child. Cutting figures on a folded sheet, leaving part of them uncut on the folded edge (Figure A) means they will stand up.

The child's simplest abstract drawing can also be done on folded paper, as long as some part of the design is left uncut along the folded edge (Figure B). The object in this case is not to make the drawing stand but to make a mirror cutout. The unfolded result is always pretty, and the child will be happy.

Chemistry

MATERIALS

glass test tubes, different sizes
wooden test tube holder, or small jars to stand test
*   tubes in*
small water pitchers
food color
Bromo Seltzer
stirrers, plastic or wooden
eye droppers, funnels, straws, salt and pepper, etc.

TO PLAY

When the child has passed the playing-in-the-sink stage, he will love anything that looks like a doctor's laboratory equipment. The test tube holder is important. I found two (wooden, hand-made wonderments) in thrift shops, but one could be taken from a used store-bought chemistry set. If nothing else, set the test tubes in a row in small peanut butter jars. You can go to a medical supply house for the test tubes and holders, or you can explain the problem to your local pharmacist, who may be remarkably helpful in supplying behind-the-counter equipment for a child.

Dress the child in a play smock. Put newspaper on a table, and put the chemistry equipment on a tray. Then let the child measure water, add food color, make bubbles with the Bromo Seltzer, stir in salt and pepper, etc. This playtime can go on for years, with less and less supervision. The child will know what he wants to make: medicine (save small bottles), magic potions, blood or whatever. If you trust the child to handle glass carefully (there will be some breakage) and grown-up ingredients, he will be engrossed.

The Impatient Child

For the child who is irritable, because of anger or some illness with intermittent pain, it helps to find an outlet for his indiscriminate energy.

I knew one boy with a toothache who found his own sedative; he cut out enough paper devils to go all the way around his room.

Make a row of apples, potatoes or onions. Pretend they are the enemy. Give the child a bean blower and let him shoot every one of them—dead! It will do him a world of good. [A bean blower can be just a short straw and small beans. Inside the house, it does make clean-up problems and should be used only on special occasions. If the vegetables are too heavy for the child to knock over, and if you're not ready to make applesauce from bruised apples, use ping-pong balls or the child's stand-up plastic cowboys and Indians.]

The impatient child likes large surfaces, long strokes, pushing away from rather than gathering in. Make a stencil out of heavy cardboard, or buy one at an art store. Fasten it well to a piece of paper, put newspapers underneath and let the child splash paint inside the stencil. Take off the stencil and lo, the child has made something in spite of himself.

Pounding out grain or corn in a mortar or bowl gives a child a way to work off pent-up feelings. The impulse to grind may be transferred from the child's teeth to a coffee mill or meat grinder. [Another possibility is to use a wet washcloth to play dog bone with a child. The child puts one end in his mouth. You get down on the floor, and with your mouth, try to get the cloth away from him. You can both make growling, tugging sounds. It's hard on the teeth, but always funny.]

When the child is feeling impatient, he cannot do anything intricate. But he also has a powerful impulse to act at any cost.

—Studies in Invalid Occupation
Susan E. Tracy, 1910

ART

Have reproductions of good pictures in the house. At least some of the child's picture books, too, should be artistically good. Take him to an art museum. Let him gaze and ask questions, but do not exhaust him with too much or too many explanations.

—Home, School and Vacation
Annie Winsor Allen, 1907

The field of art is admittedly large and complicated, but small pieces of it can provide nourishing mental food for small children. Many parents hesitate to teach "art appreciation" because they don't think they know enough about it them-

selves. But if we just keep exposing a child to whatever good art we can find, he will feel his way by himself.

Different children will prefer different subjects and different media. One child will adore any statue or sketch or painting that includes a cat; another will be intrigued by non-literal, three-eyed Picasso people. Watch your child's reactions and use what he likes to keep art alive at home. Buy postcards or inexpensive art reproductions. Keep handsome Christmas cards. If there is an art gallery nearby, go with your child and take your chances. Encourage him to draw his own version of a cat, or a three-eyed person. Let him try colored chalks, ink and, as he gets older, whittling soap or soft wood. Encourage him to stand like the statue he has just seen. Children cannot just gaze passively at art; they often need to act it out.

Take your child to any art museums in the area. A museum, because of its variety, can open the way for a child to discover his own hidden needs. What he chooses to look at may seem to have nothing to do with what you know about him. I knew one three-year-old whose parents often took her to the Metropolitan Museum of Art in New York. The parents wanted to see certain exhibits, but they always left time for Alice to choose her own favorites. She suddenly became fascinated with a naked statue of Perseus holding the gory, snake-haired head of Medusa. Instead of whisking her away from the statue, the parents let her go back time after time. They bought her a postcard photograph of the statue, looked up the Medusa myth, and told her as much as she could absorb. After a while the tattered postcard was forgotten, and Alice went on to other things. Her parents will never really know what primitive connection she was making with death, the human form or the heroic stance of the victor.

In this chapter, I have tried to give a brief cross-section of art from ancient sculpture to early-twentieth-century oil painting. Many great paintings do not reproduce well and are too staid and flat for young children. Therefore, I have leaned more heavily on pictures of statues, sketches and prints.

The picture information is written so that it can be read to a child. However, I recommend that a parent read the text before sharing the pictures, since the child may want only one spontaneous answer and have no patience with the printed page.

I have not gone beyond about 1920 for my selections, although some children find modern art (abstract sculptures, three-dimensional collages and non-realistic paintings) very interesting. My apologies to later twentieth-century artists; they simply go past my self-stated chronology.

In good art there is beauty, strength and true imagination. The sooner a child can see through an artist's eyes, the sooner he will open up a creative part of himself. But mothers must not feel they have to fill a certain quota, or attain a particular goal. Whatever art washes over a child helps him to use his eyes. And with his open eyes, a child will feed his own soul.

Statue of a Sleeping Eros. The Metropolitan Museum of
Art, Rogers Fund, 1943

Statue of a Sleeping Eros
Probably Greek, Hellenistic period, 250–150 B.C.

The boy sleeping on a rock is Eros, or Cupid, the god
of love. The ancient Greek people believed that Cupid
could make men and women fall in love just by prick-
ing them with his magic arrows. This sculptor didn't
bother with Cupid's bow, but you can see a strap across

the boy's chest that is attached to the quiver, or arrow-
holder, on his back.

Cupid was only one of many gods in the Greeks'
religion. This bronze statue makes him seem so babyish and chubby, it's hard to believe he was a god at all.
But he was, and very busy most of the time. Here he
is tired from his work and sleeping deeply. Even his
wings are folded.

The Lady and the Unicorn
French, 15th Century

A unicorn is a magical animal. He looks like a horse, but he has one very long horn growing from his forehead. People in the days of knights in armor believed that unicorns roamed in their forests, but they never could find them. The lady in this picture is lucky—she has found a gentle unicorn to be her friend.

The picture is not painted. It is made of many, many threads woven together on a huge old wooden hand-machine called a loom. Woven pictures or designs are called *tapestries*, and this one was made for a woman who was to be married to a Frenchman who lived in a *château*, or small stone castle. Châteaux were quite chilly, so the man asked the weavers to make this tapestry and others, all showing the lady and the unicorn doing different happy things, to hang on the walls of his castle to make the rooms warmer.

The lady and the unicorn seem to be floating on a garden island. She has pulled up her outer skirt so the unicorn can rest his hooves on her lap without soiling her dress. This tapestry is called "Sight," and the lady is holding up a mirror. The unicorn seems delighted to see himself, but the lady looks a little sad, as if she knows her friend is not real and will soon go away like a dream.

A friendly lion is holding up a medieval banner. Small dogs, foxes, rabbits and all kinds of flowers and grasses are woven into the fabric.

The Lady and the Unicorn—Sight. The Cluny Museum, Paris

*Moses Unlaces His Sandals to Enter the Burning Bush.
Church of San Vitale, Ravenna, Italy.*

Moses Unlaces His Sandals to Enter the Burning Bush

Italian, 6th Century

This young man is untying his sandals because God is telling him to:

Put off thy shoes from off thy feet, for the place whereon thou standest is holy ground.

—Exodus 3:5

The man's name was Moses. God wanted to talk to him, so He did something magic to make Moses come from tending his sheep and listen to Him. God started a fire in a bush in the field. Moses saw the fire —and he also saw that the bush was not being burned by it. He went close to it and heard God's voice.

Moses was Jewish, and most Jews, or Israelites, were then being held as slaves by the Egyptians. God was asking Moses to free the people of Israel and lead them back to their own land. The Egyptians were powerful, and Moses did not know how he could possibly fight them. But God kept talking to him, day after day, and eventually Moses did bring the Israelites back to their own land.

This picture is a *mosaic* on a wall in a church in Italy. Mosaics are made of many small pieces of colored glass glued together in a kind of cement. Every tiny piece is put in by hand, and each mosaic takes a long time. In this one, Moses looks unsure of himself. But even though small bits of fire are all around him, he does not seem to be afraid of being burned.

The Enraged Musician
William Hogarth (English, 1697–1764)

More than two hundred years ago, this artist watched what the people of London, England, were doing in the streets and drew this picture.

It's a noisy, silly picture. The "enraged musician" is the violinist in the window, who is holding his ears because of the noise outside.

In the street, one child is beating a drum. Another has a tile tied to a string from his waist and is dragging it across the paving stones. The tall woman in the center is probably going to trip over the string.

Another child is winding a kind of Hallowe'en noise-maker.

The woman at the right is moaning a sad song, hoping to make some money from her singing. Her baby is bawling. On the left, a knife-sharpener has set his grinding wheel down on a dog's paw, and the dog is howling.

The noise is endless: a squawking parrot, people blowing horns, and squawling cats fighting on a rooftop.

The Rhinoceros
Albrecht Dürer (German, 1471–1528)

If this rhinoceros does not look quite right to you, it is because the artist, Dürer, had never seen one. He lived in Germany, in Europe, at a time when almost no one went to Africa to look at animals or bring them back to keep in zoos.

Dürer saw a small drawing and read a letter about the rhinoceros written by a friend who had been to Africa and had seen one. Then he drew his own rhino, and because men in those days still wore armor, he made his rhinoceros into a knight in armor. Rhinos do look a little as if they were wearing armor, but they don't have metal plates covering their bodies or chain mail covering their legs.

This picture is not a drawing but a woodcut. The artist took a piece of wood and chipped away at it with different sized chisels, some very, very small. Then he put ink on the wood and a piece of paper on top of the ink. When he pulled the paper off, he had one print of his rhinoceros.

Dürer signed almost all of his pictures with just his initials, as in this one. There is always a big A, for Albrecht, and a small D underneath, for Dürer.

"The scope of the animal-painter has been greatly extended by travel and photography since the days when Dürer drew his famous rhinoceros from hearsay and a slight pencil drawing made by an eye-witness of this quite unfamiliar animal."

—How to Look at Pictures
Robert Clermont Witt, 1902

The Rhinoceros. British Museum, London

Saint Nicholas Day
Jan Steen (Dutch, 1626–1679)

In Holland children celebrate the birthday of Saint Nicholas (we call him Santa Claus) which comes almost three weeks before Christmas. This oil painting shows a big, busy Dutch family on that celebration day.

Dutch children put their shoes in front of the fireplace the night before. If they have been good, their shoes will be stuffed with small presents. If they have done something naughty, there will be only birch branches in the shoes.

In the picture, the boy at the left is crying because he got twigs. His little sister, in front, is very happy because she got a doll and other small gifts, which she has put in a pail. Her mother seems to be saying, "Come, show me your new doll." But the little girl is playing silly and won't go.

An older brother at the right is holding the baby of the family and pointing to the chimney, where Saint Nicholas climbed down. The father is sitting very quietly, right in the middle of the picture.

There are holiday breads and buns everywhere.

I think the artist liked this family.

Saint Nicholas Day. The Rijksmuseum, Amsterdam.

Don Manuel Osorio de Zuñiga
Francisco de Goya y Lucientes (Spanish, 1746–1828)

Many years ago, about the time of the American Revolution, a Spanish artist did this portrait in oil paints of a little boy from a rich Spanish family. The boy looks like a prince. In the color painting, his suit is bright red, perhaps made of velvet. His wide sash and fancy shoes are of satin.

I am sure the boy's parents told him to stand very still while the artist drew sketches of him in pencil or ink. The artist would do the oil painting later in his own studio.

At that time, children often made pets out of birds. This boy has tied a string to one leg of a magpie so the bird will not fly away. He is holding the string gently, but he looks a little unhappy, as if someone were holding onto him with a string, too. And the cats are glaring at the magpie, as though they were ready to pounce on it. The boy has smaller caged birds to play with, but they don't seem to interest him.

I think the artist wished the boy could run and play instead of standing so stiffly. But the picture isn't too serious because the artist did one silly thing. He signed the painting on the little piece of paper that the magpie is holding in his beak.

Don Manuel Osorio de Zuñiga. The Metropolitan Museum of Art, the Jules S. Bache Collection, 1949

EL S.º D.ⁿ MANVEL OSORIO MANRRIQE D ZVÑIGA S.ⁿ D GINES NACIO EN Rª LA ⅡⅡ D 178

But Grandmother, What Big Eyes You Have!
Paul Gustave Doré (French, 1832–1883)

Everybody knows about Little Red Riding Hood, but this is the only picture I've seen where the little girl has climbed in bed with the wolf disguised as her grandmother. Grandmother's nightcap has really fooled Red Riding Hood, but she is beginning to see her mistake and is pulling the covers up to protect herself.

A French artist named Gustave Doré made this picture many years ago, about the time when Abraham Lincoln was our President. Gustave Doré may have lived long before us, but he knew the story of Little Red Riding Hood, too.

The picture is a print from a wood engraving. The artist had to work slowly and carefully, because only the thin lines of wood that he did not chip away would finally make the ink picture. The carved-out places are white. To make the wolf's furry, light-and-dark face must have taken many hours.

But Grandmother, What Big Eyes You Have! The Metro-politan Museum of Art, Gift of Mrs. John Fiske, 1960

In the Circus Fernando: The Ring Master
Henri de Toulouse-Lautrec (French, 1864–1901)

The rider and trainer are enjoying their circus act, The trainer, with mustache and flowing coattails, is flicking his whip at the horse's hoof, not to hurt him but as a signal of what to do next. The performing lady, with no stirrups for her feet or any real saddle to support her, is about to do a somersault or head stand on the horse's back. Her skirt looks like a butterfly; she seems as light as air. I think the horse, trotting patiently with his head down, strong and steady, knows he has to be a good support for the lady acrobat.

The only people in the audience are men in suits and hats, no laughing children and their parents. Maybe this is only a rehearsal, and the men in suits own the circus and are making sure the butterfly lady is a good performer.

Toulouse-Lautrec, the French artist who painted this picture, did not care as much about the exact detail of what he saw as the feeling he got from watching. He was one of the first modern artists who decided not to copy everything perfectly. Because everything he drew seemed to be moving, Lautrec was often asked to design lively posters advertising Paris shows and spectacles.

*In the Circus Fernando: The Ring Master. The Art Institute
of Chicago, Gift of Tiffany and Margaret Blake*

Man With a Hat
Pablo Picasso (Spanish, 1881–1973)

Because of the way the artist drew this person, you can see three sides of the man's head at the same time. The eye part with newspaper under it is the side that is getting the most light. The middle section, with an eye, a nose and a mouth, is partly in the shade. The round black edge is the other side of the face in dark shadow.

Some people see a guitar in the picture.

The picture is a collage, which means it has things pasted onto it. First the artist drew in the lines with charcoal. Then he pasted on the newspaper pieces. The section with the mouth is painted paper, which is also glued on. Then he put back the charcoal lines that the newspaper and painted paper had covered up.

This artist, Picasso, was Spanish, but he worked in France. The newspaper he used is in French, pasted sideways. The face section talks about teeth and mouthwash; the bottom part mentions the throat and lungs.

Man with a Hat (1912).
Charcoal, ink, pasted paper, 24½ × 18⅝",
Collection, the Museum of Modern Art, New York.

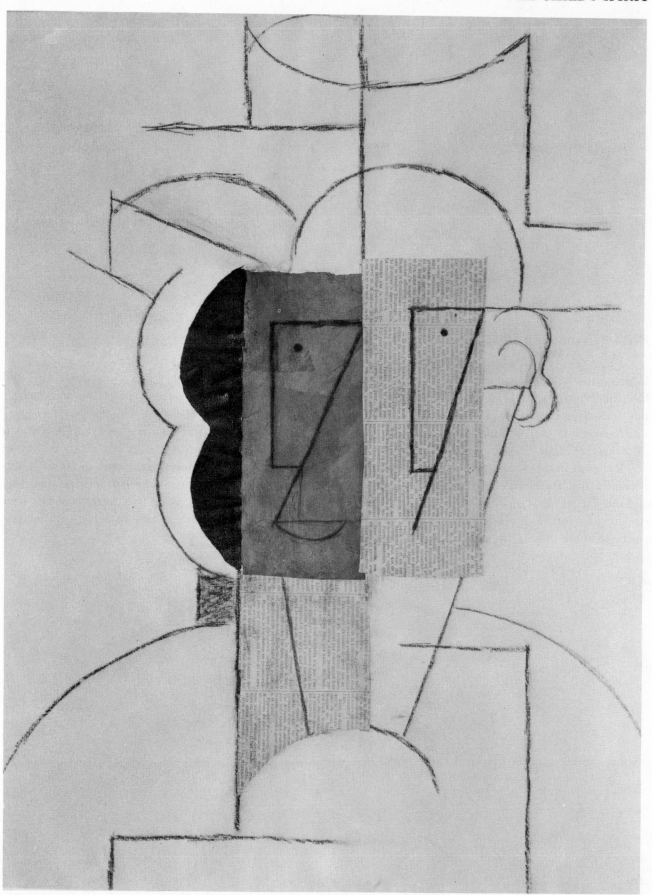

Person Throwing a Stone at a Bird
Joan Miró (Spanish, 1893–   )

I don't know why this person is throwing a stone at a bird, but the painting is so much like a silly dream that it does not worry me. The picture is surrealistic, which means it goes beyond real things. The artist, Miró, just let himself imagine.

But even imagination starts with real things. The person here is a person, even if he has only one foot and one eye. He has arms too, even if they are only a straight line with a dot in the middle. The person is at the seashore. The artist must have felt angry, because the sea is black and the sky is not sunny, and anyone throwing a stone at a bird must be angry anyway.

Miró painted this picture some years ago, but it can be called Modern Art. Very few artists now paint real-life pictures. Cameras take real pictures. Artists paint people and forms and adventures that they know are mysterious. And they know we will have to use our imagination to take ourselves into modern paintings.

Person Throwing a Stone at a Bird *(1926).*
Oil on canvas, 29 × 36¼",
Collection, the Museum of Modern Art, New York.

NATURE

A child should early see nature in its actual combinations, following his brook from its source to its mouth, exploring the elevated ridges, climbing the highest summits so that he knows the entire region in its whole.

He should watch animals and plants in their natural abodes, some basking in the sun and drinking in warmth, others hiding in shade, seeking coolness and moisture.

Mere explanations are not of interest to a child. But independent observation will awaken in him, vaguely at first, but more and more clearly, the phenomenon of the inner, constant, living unity of nature.

—The Education of Man
Friedrich Froebel, 1826

The finest of all mothercraft guides is Nature. She herself is a Mother, endowed with infinite patience, generosity and imagination. She is a quiet teacher and a steadfast friend.

Most pre–World War I children grew up close to nature: their songs, rhymes and games all reflect its influence. Some children still have nature at their doorsteps, but the majority now are prisoners of city apartments or tame suburban back yards.

Many parents feel helpless and embarrassed at how little they know about plants, animals and star formations. Our grandparents were often walking encyclopedias about flora and fauna, and they taught our parents a great deal. Some of us learned the details of the seasons, but many more were encouraged to concentrate on dancing class and book-learning rather than to play outdoors.

Our parents moved away from nature to join the "modern" world. Recently young people, and parents, have been searching for a way back. But those of us who do not want to join a corn commune in southern New Jersey should at least use what nature lore we have and reach out for more. For our children and ourselves, we need to see the sea, the sky, trees and animals.

Fortunately, young children do not need vast amounts of nature information from us. What they do need is a chance to investigate by themselves. They are much more excited by "real" things than by any commercial copy, and everything in nature is real. A child will never tire of a playground that has no man-made design.

It is less important for a young child to learn to identify fuchsias or heliotropes than it is for him to experience nature's basic elements. One of these is rain. Too often we rush children inside instead of just letting them get wet. In cool weather, I'm all for raincoats and boots. But the child who is always cautioned against rain, whatever the season, will never understand the softness of rainwater or the way leaf boats sail down gutters.

Mud is another basic, one that children love and parents hate. In fall or spring, take the child to an empty city lot, a soggy spot in the woods, or a drenched corner of the backyard. He can dig, or bulldoze, or use his hands to make mud pies. If you tell him it's the right time to get dirty, he will make wet earth—not dirt—his friend.

Fire fascinates children. Parents usually emphasize the negatives (fire burns flesh, matches are forbidden). But there are safe ways to use fire as a teaching tool. Put candles on the dinner table. If you have a fireplace, let the child gather kindling wood—broken branches in the park or dry twigs from the forest. Find an old kerosene lamp. If you have a back yard but no barbecue, dig a hole with the child's help; line it with stones and cook dinner over the fire. If you can get to a state park with fireplace facilities, go there for a picnic. Cooking hot dogs and marshmallows on skewers is exciting to a child. Lighting his own stick torches (with all due caution) is even more exhilarating.

Ice is captivating. In winter, find an ice-covered pond in the park or woods. If the ice is not thick, let the child crack the edges with a stick, poke holes, and throw stones across the surface. The joy of skating, if the ice is thick, is obviously the best of all. But ice does not have to be limited to winter. In summer, you freeze chunks of ice or just defrost the refrigerator. The city child can hammer away at the ice in a big bucket in the kitchen. The suburban child can crash the ice outside, watching it melt and spread in the sun.

Adults take rain, mud, fire and ice for granted. Children do not. They need to find out about these natural elements and feel at home with them.

Parents must only keep watch, trust a child's instincts, and not worry about keeping him spotlessly clean and dry.

Primitive nature play can begin with a six-month-old. In this chapter, however, I celebrate nature with a somewhat older child. Babies and toddlers learn to know earth and water in their own ways. A slightly older child can open himself to songs, rhymes and stories about it. He can understand using nature for games, for toys, for cooking, and how to see it in art.

When a child finds acorns under an oak tree, that is the best time for a mother to take off the acorn top and show him that he has a tiny drinking cup. When a child is at the beach and finding scallop shells, that is when she should point to the hinged edge and talk about the round up-and-down edges of the shell. Matching the information with the moment of discovery is not always possible. Even so, we must feed our children as much nature knowledge as we have, whenever we can.

I think of this chapter as an old pine chest of baked-apple smells, leaf necklaces and lost Indian arrowheads: an open chest that I hope will give children now as much peace and comfort as it has to children of generations past.

FOOD

Orange-Skin Bowls

MATERIALS
half an orange

TO MAKE

Squeeze the juice or remove the fruit from half an orange. Remove the pulp from the inside. Flatten the bottom slightly by pressing down or by making a small slice underneath.

Fill the skin with the fresh orange juice or the fruit of the orange. This is an easier way for small children to eat the fresh fruit than for them to dig it out of the rind with a spoon. It can be used as a special treat when the child is sick and especially needs fresh orange juice.

—Mother Nature's Toy Shop
Lina and Adelia Beard, 1918

Chives on the Windowsill

MATERIALS
a pot of chives from the supermarket
some rich potting soil
a pot slightly larger than the one the chives arrive in

TO MAKE

Chives are often available, and not expensive, in the market. However, they are usually potted with too little soil and in too small a pot. To keep the plant going, repot it, add soil, provide stones or shards of a broken pot on the bottom for drainage and put it by the kitchen window. Water it regularly, and all winter long you can snip off fresh chives for salads, soups, on top of cottage cheese, etc. If the leaves yellow at first, it may be a shock reaction. Give the plant time to settle down.

A child from a family with no outdoor garden has little understanding of growing food sources. A single spice plant can help him grasp the process.

A Roasted Apple

MATERIALS
a tart apple
a long string
a fireplace
a dish
sugar

TO MAKE

If you have a fireplace, try roasting apples in front of it. Tie a string to the stem of the apple. Tie the other end to something heavy or secure on the mantelpiece. Masking tape will work, or a thumbtack pushed into an inconspicuous spot on the mantel. The apple should hang in front of a low-burning fire or a grate of glowing coals.

As soon as cooking begins, twist the string and make the apple spin around slowly so that it cooks evenly on all sides. When juices begin to run from the apple, set a saucer underneath to catch them. When the apple is thoroughly cooked, pour the hot, sweet syrup over it and serve.

If it is not sweet enough, add sugar to the juice while it is still hot.

—Mother Nature's Toy Shop
Lina and Adelia Beard, 1918

HOUSEHOLD

The Child's Own Plant

Putting a plant in the child's room will make nature more real to him. Telling him you trust him to care for the plant (with help when he needs it) can really spur his interest.

Any small dime store plant will do. Make sure there is a wide dish underneath in case the child over-waters or spills. Give him his own small watering pitcher.

A plant that grows quickly works better than, for example, a sedentary cactus.

Sprout an avocado pit, telling the child in advance that you will plant it for him once it is ready.

Take three- or four-inch cuttings from a plant in the house, or ask a generous neighbor for some. A plant that propagates easily (e.g., Wandering Jew, a common house plant, the most familiar kind having purple leaves with silver streaks) should be used. Let the child watch the cuttings begin to send out roots in a glass of water. Then pot them for him. In no time, he may have a cascading plant on his own windowsill.

MUSIC

Now the Day Is Over

This song is a simple nighttime prayer. It reassures the child that the sun always goes down, that the evening darkness never lasts.

The pattern of light and dark, day and night, is a mystery. A quiet evening song, repeated and repeated, gives them a sense of the sureness of nature's ways.

Sabine Baring-Gould.

J. Barnby.

1. Now the day is o - ver, Night is draw - ing nigh,............
2. Now the dark - ness gath - ers, Stars be - gin to peep,............
3. Je - sus, give the wea - ry Calm and sweet re - pose,............
4. Thro' the long night-watch - es May Thine an - gels spread..........

Shad - ows of the eve - ning Steal a - cross the sky.
Birds and beasts and flow - ers Soon will be a - sleep.
With Thy ten - d'rest bless - ing May our eye - lids close.
Their white wings a - bove me, Watch - ing round my bed.

eve - ning steal a - cross the sky.

Eency Weency Spider

This is a traditional Southern fingerplay song. The spider is a crawling thumb and index finger. The rain is hands flopping down. The sun is the hands making a circle. Then up crawl the fingers again.

Een - cy ween - cy spi - der went up the wa - ter spout,

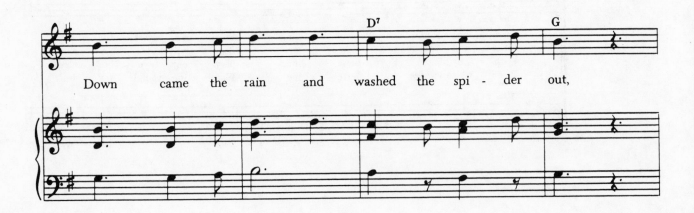

Down came the rain and washed the spi - der out,

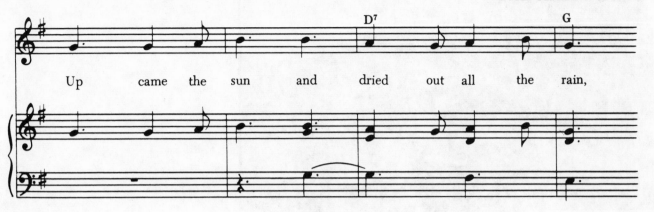

Up came the sun and dried out all the rain,

So the een - cy ween - cy spi - der went up the spout a - gain.

RHYMES

If a mother and child have just been to the zoo or the woods and have seen a wood-chuck, this jingle is perfect. If not, the silliness still works.

The Woodchuck

How Much Wood?

How much wood would a woodchuck chuck
If a woodchuck could chuck wood?
He would chuck as much wood as a woodchuck could
    chuck
If a woodchuck could chuck wood.

—Mother Goose

N.B.: *A woodchuck is a ground hog. The name woodchuck has American Indian origins and has nothing to do with either wood or the chucking of it.*

The Little Turtle

Add as much fingerplaying to this as you want. Make the turtle swim with your fingers, climb, snap and finally catch the child.

There was a little turtle.
He lived in a box.
He swam in a puddle.
He climbed on the rocks.

He snapped at a mosquito.
He snapped at a flea.
He snapped at a minnow.
And he snapped at me.

He caught the mosquito.
He caught the flea.
He caught the minnow.
But he didn't catch me.

—Collected Poems
Vachel Lindsay, 1920

STORIES

The Little Tree That Longed for Other Leaves

There was once a little tree in the woods that was covered with needles instead of leaves.

"All my tree friends have beautiful green leaves, but I have only sharp needles, so sharp that no one will touch me. If I could have a magic wish, I would wish for leaves of pure gold."

The next morning, the tree woke early and found itself covered with gle ning, golden leaves.

"Ah!" said the little tree, "how grand I am! No other tree is dressed in gold."

That evening, a peddler with a great sack and a long beard passed by. He saw the glittering leaves. Quickly he picked them all, stuffed them in his sack, and hurried away.

"Alas!" cried the little tree, cold and bare. "All my golden leaves are gone. I am ashamed to stand among the other trees. If only I had another wish, I would ask for leaves of glass."

The next morning, the little tree again woke early to find itself covered with shining leaves of glass.

"Now I am happy," said the tree. "No tree in the woods glistens like me."

But there came a fierce storm and driving wind. It struck the tree, and in a moment all the glass leaves lay shattered on the ground.

"Oh my beautiful glass leaves!" moaned the little tree. "They lie broken while all the other trees are still dressed in their pretty foliage. Oh! If I had one more wish, I would ask for green leaves."

When the tree woke in the morning, it laughed merrily, because it was covered in fresh, green leaves.

"Now I will not be ashamed any more," said the tree. "I am as pretty as all my tree friends."

But along came a goat, looking for food. He saw the little tree and the crisp new leaves, and the goat nibbled and nibbled until he had eaten all the leaves and some of the stems and tender shoots as well.

"Alas!" cried the little tree, bare and miserable. "I want no more leaves. Not gold ones, or glass ones, or green ones, or any kind. If only I could have my needles back again, I would never complain any more."

The little tree cried itself to sleep that night. But in the morning sunshine, it felt as joyful as a tree can feel. It was a pine tree again, covered with needles.

The next time you go in the woods, you may find the little tree. But do not touch it, because it pricks.

—*Friedrich Rückert, 1788–1866*
(adapted)

The Two Frogs

Once upon a time in the country of Japan there lived two frogs. One made his home in a ditch near the town of Osaka, on the seacoast. The other dwelled in a clear stream which ran through the city of Kyoto, where the Imperial Mikado had his palace. The frogs lived a great distance apart, but they decided at about the same time that they wanted to see a little of the world. The frog who lived in Kyoto wanted to visit the seaport city of Osaka. The frog who lived in Osaka wished to go to the royal city of Kyoto.

One fine morning, the frogs began their separate journeys along the road that led from the one city to the other. Neither frog knew much about traveling, and halfway between the two cities each discovered there was a mountain to be climbed. It took them a long time and a great many tiring hops, but at last they met each other at the top.

Each surprised the other, and they sat there awhile just looking at each other. Then they began to talk. The more they talked, the more they were delighted to find out that they were alike; each of them wanted to learn a little more about his native country.

"What a pity we are not bigger," said the Osaka frog, resting with his friend in a cool, damp place by the side of the road. "If we were bigger, we could see both towns from here and decide if we should travel on."

"Oh, that's easy," said the Kyoto frog. "If we stand on our hind legs and hold on to each other, then we can each look at the towns we are going to."

Since frogs have trouble standing by themselves, the Osaka frog was very pleased by this idea. He jumped up and put his webbed arms on his friend's shoulders. They stretched themselves as high as possible. The Osaka frog turned his nose toward Kyoto. The Kyoto frog turned his nose toward Osaka. For a long time, they stood and looked, not knowing they were making a silly mistake.

Frogs have big rolling eyes that lie far back from their noses. The two frogs had their noses pointed in the right direction, but their eyes were looking backward. Each frog was seeing the city he had just come from.

"Dear me!" cried the Osaka frog. "Kyoto looks exactly like my city. It is certainly not worth such a long journey. I think I shall go home."

"Dear me!" exclaimed the Kyoto frog. "Osaka seems to be exactly like Kyoto." They let go of each other's shoulders and fell down in the grass.

The frogs said a fond farewell to each other and turned around to go back home. It just so happens that the cities of Osaka and Kyoto are as different as two cities can be, but the two frogs believed, to the end of their days, that they were as alike as two peas in a pod.

—*Andrew Lang, 1844–1912*
(adapted)

PLAYTIME

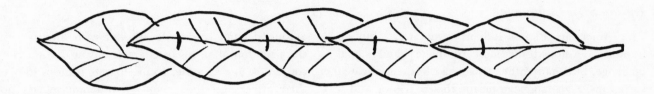

Leaf Chains and Acorn Chains

Collect large leaves. Link them together with short, thin pieces of twigs or pine needles. The chains can be necklaces, belts or garlands for the child's head. Leaf chains are delicate, so do not try them with a very young child.

Acorn chains are even simpler. In the fall, collect different kinds and sizes of acorns. (The various types of oak trees yield very different acorns.) With a strong needle and heavy thread, you can easily string them together. In the open air, acorns dry well and last a long time.

Remove the peas. Keep the pod open with two or more braces made of toothpicks. Fill the sink or give the child a wide pan of water set on newspapers. These boats are tippy and should not be tried until the child is old enough to move them gently.

A paper flag attached to a toothpick can be added at the bow.

—Mother Nature's Toy Shop
Lina and Adelia Beard, 1918

Pea-pod Canoe

MATERIALS
several pea pods
toothpicks
water

TO MAKE AND PLAY
Open the pod carefully along its straightest edge.

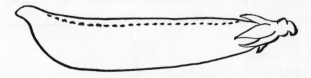

Cut open the pea pod along dotted line.

Indian Sign Language

The American Plains Indians (who were buffalo hunters) developed the most complete hand signal language, but many other tribes had less complicated variations. Sign language meant that a Kiowa and a Cheyenne, who had different spoken languages, could hold long conversations without words. It meant that a council chief could silently and with dignity gain the attention of all his listeners. It meant that warriors could talk to each other from separate hilltops to plan their attacks on the enemy. Sign language was not invented in order to talk to the White Man. The Indians needed it to talk to each other.

HUNGRY

DRINK
Make a cup of your right hand.
Move your hand to your mouth.
(This gesture can also mean water.)

DRINK

HUNGRY
Hold your right hand palm up.
Cut across your stomach several times.
(i.e., empty, cut in half.)

DAY

Hold both hands palm down.
Make a night shadow by crossing the right hand over
 the left.
Turn palms up to show that night is over.

SIT DOWN

Make fists of both hands, right over left.
Push downward.
(The sign for planting is done the same way.)

ART

Shells

The first shell in this picture is called a nautilus. It is real. The second is a snail shell, but it is not real. It is made of metal and was used long ago as a drinking cup.

Pictures 3 and 4 are scallop shells, the outside, and the inside. A scallop is a sea animal that lives inside two curved, ridged, hinged shells. Some scallop shells are big enough to use for dishes.

Pictures 5, 6 and 7 are scallop-shell designs, carved out of wood or marble or made of plaster to decorate columns in houses or to go over fancy doors. Marble or stone scallop basins are often used in outdoor fountains.

Long ago in the Middle Ages, men known as pilgrims often made long journeys to the Holy Land, to the place where Jesus was born. On their journey, they often wore a scallop badge. When people along the way saw the badge, they would invite the tired pilgrims into their houses to eat and rest.

Shells are ocean houses for small creatures of the sea, and they are all beautiful. Since cavemen first painted horses on the walls of their caves, people have known that nature is something they want to use in their lives and in their art.

1

2

3

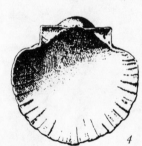

4

5

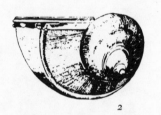

6

7

Lions

In ancient days, when designers wanted to make a handsome animal statue, they often chose the King of Beasts, the lion. Artists saw the male lion's beautiful thick mane and strong muscles, the proud way he held his head. He seemed the perfect animal to protect a building or to rule over a royal garden.

The first drawing here is of a real lion, fierce, tail held high, walking quickly on his heavily padded feet. The second picture is an Egyptian lion sculpture. He looks much more stiff and less real than the first lion. His mane is flat, as though it has been brushed back. His tail is held low. But he too looks proud, with the fancy ribbons tied around his stomach. In fact, he is only a half-statue. He was carved into the wall of an Egyptian temple, as decoration and a token of good luck.

When important people died, artists sometimes put a sleeping lion on top of the tomb. The third picture is a lion sculpted to protect a monument to the Roman Catholic Pope Clement XIII, in St. Peter's Cathedral in Rome, Italy.

In front of the huge New York City Public Library there is a quiet, watchful stone lion on either side of the long steps that lead up to the building. Lions still remind people that certain places are special, places to honor and take care of.

OUTDOORS

English Sparrow

He fears neither man nor beast, multiplies as fast as the rabbit and chirps as cheerfully in reeking gutters as in the prettiest gardens.

—Birds Every Child Should Know
Neltje Blanchan, 1907

Most birds need to live in quiet places, close to nature. Not the English sparrow. He can make his nest on top of city buildings and eat from any garbage can.

In the country, he frightens other, prettier birds away from their nests and pushes them away from bird feeders and berry bushes. People in the country think he is a pest and want him to go away.

The fact is, the English sparrow wouldn't be here at all if we hadn't brought him here. A hundred years ago, some people in Brooklyn, a part of New York City, were worrying about the inchworms that were eating up their trees. They brought a flock of English sparrows over from England by boat, hoping the birds would eat the inchworms. The sparrows did, but soon there were so many of them that they went to make new homes in all the nearby cities and states.

This foreign visitor is still a problem in the country, but at least he keeps us company in the city. You will see him outside, on the sidewalk or on the lawn, gray-brown, small and noisy.

This notorious bird never makes a 'musical' sound.

—Birds in the Bush
Bradford Torrey, 1885

The Robin

One bright morning early in March, you go outside and hear the cheery song of the first robin of the spring. Perched in a leafless tree, he sings as though he would pour out his very soul.

—Birds in the Bush
Bradford Torrey, 1885

The American robin is a big, friendly creature. He is special because he flies back from his warm winter vacation earlier than almost any other bird.

In the northern states in early April, you can see the mother and father birds making a grassy tree nest (not a very neat one, but comfortable) for the turquoise-blue eggs the mother robin will lay. She warms them. The eggs hatch, and the mother and father work all day long to find enough earth worms to feed the fledglings. By late June, which is still early in the summer, the baby birds are out of the nest, flying and hopping around to find their own food.

Our robin got his name by mistake. There are many songs and poems about Cock Robin and Robin Redbreast, but these were made up long ago by people in England, across the Atlantic Ocean. Their poems were about a small red-breasted bird there, also called a robin. When English people first began to come to this country, they missed their robin. Then they saw our big songbird—who also had a red vest—and they named him robin, to make themselves feel more at home in a new land.

Wild Flowers

Wild flowers are beautiful. Goldenrod, blue chicory and pink clover color the countryside in summer. But farmers call them weeds because they may try to take over a field he has plowed and planted. They can crowd out and kill the young plants the farmer is trying to grow.

Some wild flowers are plants that once were grown only in gardens. Over the years, the seeds have been blown by the wind or carried by birds to empty fields and roadsides. Two such flowers are Queen Anne's lace (wild carrot) and the white daisy.

QUEEN ANNE'S LACE

From Europe, it has come to spread its delicate wheels over our summer landscape. East of the Mississippi, whole fields are whitened by them.
> —Wild Flowers Worth Knowing
> *Neltje Blanchan, 1917*

You can find this white, circular flower along any rail-road track, in abandoned city lots and at the edges of country roads. Each one is actually a bouquet of small, delicate blossoms in a flat-topped cluster. The leaves are fine and fringy. The stem has stiff hairs and a deep, fleshy root. It flowers from June to September.

If you want to pick Queen Anne's lace—or any wild flower—have a bucket of lukewarm water ready. They do not last long out of water.

Queen Anne was apparently given to wearing exquisite lace in intricate medallion patterns.
> —Handbook of Nature Study
> *Anna Botsford Comstock, 1911*

COMMON DAISY

The white daisy has many names: whiteweed, oxeye daisy, marguerite, love me–love me not. It grows all across the United States, but especially in the North and Midwest. It will spring up on roadsides, in meadows, or in vacant city lots. The petals are white. The yellow centers are hundreds of minute florets huddled together in a green cup. The leaves are narrow and coarsely toothed. The daisy season is long—from May to November.

The English origin of the name of this triumphant foreigner is Day's Eye, for it closes at nightfall and opens with the dawn.

—Wild Flowers Worth Knowing
Neltje Blanchan, 1917

Water Play

Teach the meaning of pond, brook, stream and bridge, if you can, by artificial ponds, brooks, streams and bridges, devised with the child's help.

—Bookless Lessons for the Teacher-Mother
Ella Frances Lynch, 1922

In summer, if you have a back yard, let the child run a hose (turned down to a trickle) on a downhill slope—not through grass but along the dirt borders of bushes or plants. The child will deepen gullies, make log boats and dams. He will line harbors with stones and invent docks. If a mother decides not to worry about water soppage and muddy clothes, the child can busy himself for hours.

If you have no back yard and no hose, you can give the housebound child a smaller indoor version. With a wide, deep pan or fish bowl, some gravel or sand, a spoon, stones and some sticks or small boats, the child will stir up his own land formations. Put down plenty of newspaper, preferably in the kitchen, and keep everything on a large tray. Give him a washcloth to mop up after himself.

Imbedding a permanent nature interest in the young child can be a safeguard for him in the tempestuous years to come, during which the mind tends to become centered on self.

—Bookless Lessons for the Teacher-Mother
Ella Frances Lynch, 1922

TO ANY READER

As from the house your mother sees
You playing round the garden trees,
So you may see, if you will look
Through the windows of this book,
Another child, far, far away,
And in another garden, play.
But do not think you can at all,
By knocking on the window, call
That child to hear you. He intent
Is all on his play business bent.
He does not hear; he will not look,
Nor yet be lured out of this book.
For, long ago, the truth to say,
He has grown up and gone away,
And it is but a child of air
That lingers in the garden there.

—A Child's Garden of Verses
Robert Louis Stevenson, 1885

Bibliography

Adeline, M. Jules, *Adeline's Art Dictionary*. New York, D. Appleton and Co., 1905.

Agay, Denes, *Best Loved Songs of the American People*. New York, Doubleday & Company, Inc., 1975.

Allen, Annie Winsor, *Home, School and Vacation*. Boston, Houghton Mifflin Co., The Riverside Press, 1907.

American Farm and Home Cyclopædia. New York, F. M. Lupton Co., 1887.

Aries, Philippe, *Centuries of Childhood*. New York, Vintage Books, published by Alfred A. Knopf, Inc., and Random House, Inc., 1960.

Arnold, Arnold, *Pictures and Stories From Forgotten Children's Books*. New York, Dover Publications, Inc., 1969.

Ashton-Warner, Sylvia, *Teacher*. New York, Bantam Books, published by arrangement with Simon and Schuster, Inc., 1963.

Barnes' Historical Series, *A Brief History of the United States*. New York, A. S. Barnes & Co., 1871.

Baring-Gould, William S., and Ceil Baring-Gould, *The Annotated Mother Goose*. New York, Bramhall House, a division of Clarkson Potter, Inc., 1962.

Beard, Lina and Adelia, *Mother Nature's Toy Shop*. New York, Charles Scribner's Sons, 1918.

Beecher, Catherine E., and Harriet Beecher Stowe, *The American Woman's Home*. New York, J. B. Ford & Co., 1869.

Blake, Mary, *Twenty-Six Hours a Day*. D. Lothrop & Co., 1883.

Blanchan, Neltje, *Birds Every Child Should Know*. New York, Doubleday, Page & Co., 1907.

Blanchan, Neltje, *Wild Flowers Worth Knowing*, adapted by ASA Don Dickinson, from *Nature's Garden*. New York, Little Nature Library, Doubleday, Page & Co., 1917.

Child, Mrs., *The American Frugal Housewife*, originally published Boston, 1836; facsimile edition, New York, Harper & Row, 1972.

Chukovsky, Kornei, *From Two to Five*. Los Angeles, University of California Press, 1963.

Coleman, Satis N., *Creative Music for Children*. New York, G. P. Putnam's Sons, 1922.

Comstock, Anna Botsford, *Handbook of Nature-Study*. Ithaca, New York, The Comstock Publishing Co., 1911.

Crane, Walter (1845–1915), *The Baby's Bouquet*. London, Frederick Warne & Co., Ltd., 1879.

Crane, Walter, *The Baby's Opera*. London, Frederick Warne & Co., Ltd., 1877.

Croy, Mae Savell, *Putnam's Household Handbook*. New York, G. P. Putnam's Sons, 1916.

Dodson, Dr. Fitzhugh, *How to Parent*. Los Angeles, Nash Publishing, 1970.

Fischer, Louis, M.D., *The Health Care of the Growing Child*. New York, Funk and Wagnalls, 1915.

Froebel, Friedrich, *The Education of Man*. New York, International Education Series, D. Appleton & Co., 1887.

Gardner, Helen, *Art Throughout the Ages.* New York, Harcourt, Brace and Co., 1926.

Gibbs, Charlotte M., *Household Textiles.* Boston, Whitcomb & Barrows, 1912.

Griffith, J. P., Crozer, M.D., *Diseases of Infants and Children.* W. B. Saunders Company, 1919.

Hillyer, V. M., *Kindergarten at Home.* New York, Blake & Taylor Co., 1911.

Holt, John, *How Children Learn.* New York, Dell Publishing Co., 1967.

Ives, Burl, *The Burl Ives Song Book.* New York, Ballantine Books, 1953.

Johnson, George Ellsworth, *Education by Play and Games.* Boston, Ginn & Co., 1907.

Kittredge, Mabel Hyde, *The Home and Its Management.* New York, The Century Co., 1917.

Laurel, Alicia Bay, *Living on the Earth.* New York, Vintage Books, a division of Random House, 1970.

Lear, Edward, *Nonsense Omnibus.* New York, Frederick Warne & Co., 1943.

Leslie, Miss, *American Girl's Book.* Boston, Munroe & Francis, 1838.

Lomax, John and Alan, *American Ballads & Folksongs.* New York, The Macmillan Co., 1934.

Lynch, Ella Frances, *Bookless Lessons for the Teacher-Mother.* New York, The Macmillan Co., 1922.

Mead, Margaret, *Blackberry Winter; My Earlier Years.* New York, William Morrow & Co., Inc., 1972.

Milne, A. A., *When We Were Very Young.* New York, E. P. Dutton & Co., 1924.

Montessori, Maria, *Dr. Montessori's Own Handbook.* New York, Frederick A. Stokes Co., 1914.

Newell, William Wells, *Games and Songs of American Children,* originally published by Harper and Brothers, 1883; reprint, New York, Dover Publications, Inc., 1963.

Olcott, Francis Jenkins, *Good Stories for Great Holidays.* Cambridge, Houghton Mifflin Co., The Riverside Press, 1914.

Opie, Peter and Iona, *The Oxford Book of Children's Verse.* Oxford and New York, Oxford University Press, 1973.

Pfaundler, Dr. M., and Dr. A. Schlossmann, *The Diseases of Children.* Philadelphia, J. B. Lippincott Co., 1908.

Piaget, Jean, *The Origins of Intelligence in Children.* New York, W. W. Norton & Co., Inc., 1952.

Pines, Maya, *Revolution in Learning.* New York, Harper & Row, 1966.

Randolph, Mrs. Mary, *The Virginia Housewife,* originally published in 1860 by E. H. Butler and Co., Philadelphia; reprint, New York, Avenel Books, a division of Crown Publishers, Inc., by arrangement with the Valentine Museum, Richmond, Va., 1971.

Read, Mary L., *The Mothercraft Manual.* Boston, Little, Brown and Co., 1916.

Reinach, S., *The Story of Art Throughout the Ages.* New York, Charles Scribner's Sons, 1905.

Ross, David, ed., *Poetry for Children.* New York, Grosset & Dunlap, 1970.

Rossetti, Christina, *Sing-Song,* originally published by George Routledge and Sons, London, 1872, reprint, New York, Dover Publications, Inc., 1968.

Songs That Never Grow Old. New York, Syndicate Publishing Co. and North American Publishing Co., 1909.

Spock, Dr. Benjamin, *Baby and Child Care.* New York, Pocket Books, a division of Simon and Schuster, Inc., 1945.

Stevenson, Robert Louis, *A Child's Garden of Verses.* New York, Charles Scribner's Sons, 1905. Illustrations by Jessie Willcox Smith.

Torrey, Bradford, *Birds in the Bush.* Boston and New York, Houghton, Mifflin and Co., 1885.

Tracy, Susan E., *Studies in Invalid Occupation.* Boston, Whitcomb & Barrows, 1910.

Tyrrell, Charles A., M.D., *The Royal Road to Health.* New York. Tyrrell's Hygenic Institute, 1908.

Weaver, Laurence, *The House and Its Equipment.* New York, Charles Scribner's Sons, 1912.

Wessells, Katherine Tyler, *The Golden Song Book.* New York, Golden Press, 1945.

West, John D., M.D., *Maidenhood and Motherhood.* Wilkesbarre, Pa., Pennsylvania Book Co., 1888.

Wierc, Albert E., *Songs the Whole World Sings.* New York, D. Appleton & Co., 1915.

Winn, Marie, and Allan Miller, *Fireside Book of Children's Songs.* New York, Simon and Schuster, 1966.

Winn, Marie, and Mary Ann Porcher, *The Playgroup Book.* New York, The Macmillan Co., 1967.

Witt, Robert Clermont, *How to Look at Pictures.* London, George Bell and Sons, 1902.

Yolen, Jane, *The Fireside Song Book of Birds and Beasts.* New York, Simon and Schuster, 1972.

ABOUT THE AUTHOR

Margaretta Lundell was born in New York City and grew up in New Jersey. She spent her junior year of college studying at the Sorbonne in Paris, received her B.A. from Smith College, and then attended Yale Drama School. She later worked for literary agents in New York while writing short stories, including one for Cosmopolitan.

Mrs. Lundell now lives in New York with her six-year-old son Erik and does free-lance work for The Reader's Digest *while actively engaged in mothercraft.*